SPIRITUAL WARFARE

SELF-STUDY BIBLE COURSE

SPIRITUAL WARFARE

SELF-STUDY BIBLE COURSE

Mary K. Baxter

WHITAKER
HOUSE

SPIRITUAL WARFARE SELF-STUDY BIBLE COURSE

ISBN: 978-1-60374-492-8 • eBook ISBN: 978-1-60374-527-7
Printed in Colombia
© 2012 by Mary K. Baxter

Whitaker House
1030 Hunt Valley Circle
New Kensington, PA 15068
www.whitakerhouse.com

Library of Congress Cataloging-in-Publication Data
Baxter, Mary K.
  Spiritual warfare self-study bible course / by Mary Baxter.
     p. cm.
  Summary:"A self-guided Bible study course providing an overview of the origin and nature of spiritual warfare and how Christian believers can overcome Satan through their authority in Christ and the power of the Holy Spirit"—Provided by publisher.
  ISBN 978-1-60374-492-8 (trade pbk. : alk. paper) 1. Spiritual warfare—Textbooks. I. Title.
  BV4509.5.B397 2012
  235'.4—dc23
                    2012020180

13 14 15 16 17 18 19 20 21 22 ꟽ 32 31 30 29 28 27 26 25 24

Contents

Part V: Final Victory

PREFACE

It was nearly forty years ago that Jesus first revealed to me the tactics that Satan (the devil) uses in his attempts to destroy humanity and how people need to be delivered from these onslaughts. The Lord warned me that Satan's assaults on the earth would increase as he released more demons from hell to cause rebellion and destruction.

All of us who have received Jesus Christ as Savior and Lord need to know how to wage warfare against our spiritual enemy. As we learn to do so, we can protect ourselves from his inevitable attacks and fulfill what God, our heavenly Father, has called us to do through Christ. *"For we are [God's] workmanship, created in Christ Jesus for good works, which God prepared beforehand that we should walk in them"* (Ephesians 2:10). Spiritual warfare is not just for preachers or other spiritual leaders. I began my journey of learning about spiritual warfare as a concerned mother and homemaker, and I know the principles in this book apply to everyone.

The *Spiritual Warfare Self-Study Bible Course* will show you, step-by-step, the reality of the spiritual realm and how to defeat the enemy. Be encouraged! God is all-powerful, and He has provided everything you need to stand strong against Satan. The Lord has given me visions and revelations of the spiritual realm, and I have seen the reality of spiritual warfare that takes place behind the scenes of our physical world, including battles between angels and demons. I have observed how the enemy and his evil spirits ensnare people. But, most important, I have seen the power of our Victor, Jesus Christ, and the glory of God, which protect us and release us from those snares.

When God gives us visions and revelations, it is His way of allowing us to take a glimpse into the invisible realm of His omnipotent power. I have learned to overcome the enemy by understanding the nature of the spiritual realm, exercising authority over Satan, and persevering in intercessory prayer. I have prayed against demonic strongholds, and I have witnessed the miraculous hand of God heal and deliver many people. You can experience spiritual freedom and effectively wage spiritual warfare as you understand and act upon these truths:

1. **Satan attempts to attack all believers, in one way or another.** *"Be sober, be vigilant; because your adversary the devil walks about like a roaring lion, seeking whom he may devour. Resist him, steadfast in the faith"* (1 Peter 5:8–9). He tries to prevent us from living the abundant life that our heavenly Father desires for us through Jesus Christ. *"The thief [Satan] does not come except to steal, and to kill, and to destroy. I [Jesus] have come that they may have life, and that they may have it more abundantly"* (John 10:10).

2. **We can stand firm against Satan to protect our spiritual health and to support the development of our faith.** We can loosen the devil's chains and cast down demonic strongholds through the weapons of spiritual warfare God has given us. (See Ephesians 6:10–19.)

3. **Satan attempts to deceive the whole world and prevent people from believing in Jesus and receiving God's help.** (See, for example, Revelation 12:9.) Through the compassion of Jesus and the power of the Holy Spirit, we can fight on behalf of others whom Satan is attacking, or has already oppressed or possessed, and help set them free.

4. **Jesus has already won the ultimate victory over Satan!** (See, for example, Colossians 2:15.) As God's children and joint heirs with Christ (see Romans 8:16–17), we can thwart Satan's schemes and bring the kingdom of God to earth, as it is in heaven.

5. **We can live in the fullness of the Spirit, enjoying fellowship with God our Father and all that He has provided for us.** (See, for example, 1 John 1:2–4; Romans 8:32; 14:17.)

Ephesians 6:12 says, *"For we do not wrestle against flesh and blood, but against principalities, against powers, against the rulers of the darkness of this age, against spiritual hosts of wickedness in the heavenly places."* These wicked spiritual entities must be put under Jesus' feet through prayer and faith in God's Word. (See 1 Corinthians 15:25.) We have the authority and power to do this in Jesus' name because of the new covenant we have entered into with God our heavenly Father through Jesus' death on the cross and His triumphant resurrection.

Let's pray together as we begin this Bible course, that we will become equipped to wage spiritual warfare and overcome Satan through the authority and power of Jesus:

Heavenly Father,

Thank You for these dear ones whom You have called to be Your children, and through whom You desire to bring Your kingdom on earth. Open their hearts and minds to learn from Your Word about the spiritual realm in which we live. Show them how they can stand strong against Satan, as well as his demons. Thank You that we have both authority and power through Your Son Jesus Christ to overcome the enemy's schemes and attacks against us and our loved ones and to put Satan's demons under Jesus' feet. Thank you that we can live the abundant life Jesus came to give us. I ask You to mightily prepare and use all who study Your Word through this Bible course for these important purposes in Your kingdom. In Jesus' precious name, amen.

—Dr. Mary K. Baxter

Introduction

Using This Bible Course

Overview

Purpose:

The *Spiritual Warfare Self-Study Bible Course* is designed to give students an overview of the nature and realm of spiritual warfare. It teaches how believers can effectively battle Satan through the authority they have in Christ Jesus and the power they receive through the Holy Spirit.

Bible Translation:

The main Bible translation used in this course is the *New King James Version* (NKJV). When another Bible version is referred to, it is indicated in parentheses. These include (KJV) for the King James Version, (NIV) for the *New International Version*, and (NASB) for the *New American Standard Bible*.

Components of Each Study

Introduction:

A brief orientation to the theme by author Mary Baxter precedes each lesson.

Memory Verse or Passage:

Each study has a corresponding memory verse or passage that the student should memorize before going on to the next study.

Study Questions:

Each question is followed by one or more Scripture references in parentheses that will enable the student to answer it. (Note: This doesn't necessarily mean that every Scripture applicable to the topic has been listed. Those included are either representative or most apparent for deriving the answer.) If a verse has *a* or *b* after it, such as "Romans 8a" or "Romans 8b," this means the answer is found in the first part of the verse, "a," or the second part, "b."

After reading the Bible passage, the student should write the answer in the line or lines provided after each question. Some questions have multiple parts, often indicated by (a), (b), (c), and so forth.

Keep in mind that some Scriptures are given more than once throughout the lessons because there is naturally some overlapping of topics or because a passage may apply to more than one aspect of spiritual warfare.

For Further Reflection:

Questions and statements for further consideration related to the lesson are included at the very end of each study.

Study Helps

Answer Key:

Correct answers and additional explanations, as necessary, are provided in the Answer Key section at the back of this study course. The student's answers should reflect the content of the Answer Key, though the wording may differ slightly.

Glossary:

For convenience, words in the text that are defined in the Glossary at the back of this study course have an asterisk (*) next to them.

Part I

The Realm of the Spirit

God Is Spirit

Introduction

There is so much more to life than the physical world we experience through our five senses. Yes, we live in a material world and inhabit physical bodies, but our lives are also greatly affected by an unseen spiritual realm. The physical world around us exists *within* this spiritual realm. When we recognize this fact, we will begin to comprehend the domain of the spirit and the nature of spiritual warfare. We will have a greater awareness of the spiritual powers that influence the physical world we live in—forces that are both positive and negative. We will also recognize the origin of various problems we have encountered in life that we have had difficulty overcoming. In studies 1 and 2 of this Bible course, we will take an overview of the character and purposes of God our Creator* and the nature of the spiritual and physical realms in which we exist.

Memory Passage:

True worshippers will worship [God] the Father in spirit and truth; for the Father is seeking such to worship Him. God is Spirit, and those who worship Him must worship in spirit and truth.

(John 4:23–24)

Study Questions

1. What did God create? (Genesis 1:1; Jeremiah 10:12; Acts 17:24)

2. From where does God rule? (Psalm 103:19; Ephesians 1:20)

_____

3. How is God described by the apostle John? (John 4:24)

_____

4. List two of God's central qualities. (Leviticus 19:2; 1 John 4:8, 16)

(1) _____ (2) _____

5. What is one characteristic of God as a spiritual Being? (Colossians 1:15a)

_____

6. What are two attributes of God's spiritual nature? (Romans 1:20b)

(1) _____ (2) _____

7. The Bible reveals that God is triune*, meaning "three in one." Who are the three persons of the Trinity? (Matthew 3:16–17; John 1:1, 14–18; 2 Corinthians 13:14; 1 Peter 1:2)

(1) _____ (2) _____ (3) _____

8. Which persons of the Trinity participated in the process of creation? (Genesis 1:1, 2b; John 1:1, 3; Colossians 1:15–16)

_____

9. What were human beings created to reflect? (Genesis 1:26a)

_____

10. List the three aspects of human beings by completing the following:

    1 Thessalonians 5:23b: *"May your whole* _____ , _____ , *and*

    _____ *be preserved blameless at the coming of our Lord Jesus Christ."*

11. What is the essence of human beings, which returns to God after we die? (Ecclesiastes 12:7)

    _____

12. In what two ways are human beings to worship God? (John 4:23–24)

    (1) _____ (2) _____

13. What two categories do all created things fall under? (Colossians 1:16)

    (1) _____ (2) _____

14. Which is greater: God and that which is spiritual, or that which is earthly and/or physical? (2 Chronicles 20:6; Psalm 103:19; 1 Corinthians 9:11)

    _____

15. Besides human beings (who are made in God's image and likeness), what is another type of spiritual being that was created by God? (Genesis 28:12b; Nehemiah 9:6; Hebrews 1:6; Revelation 7:11)

    _____

16. Are these other spiritual beings to be worshipped? Why or why not? (Colossians 2:18; Revelation 22:8–9)

    _____

17. What is one significant role of God's angels? (Hebrews 1:13–14)

    _____

18. What is one way in which God's invisible spiritual attributes can be recognized by human beings living on earth? (Romans 1:20)

_____

19. In the Old Testament, what did the tabernacle and the religious practices that were given to the Israelites by God represent? (Hebrews 8:4–5; Colossians 2:16–17)

_____

_____

20. What does the Spirit of God* search out? (1 Corinthians 2:10b)

_____

21. Who can be considered "sons [children] of God"? (Romans 8:14)

_____

For Further Reflection

+ Do you think of yourself as a spiritual being dwelling in a physical body? Why or why not?

+ In what ways could acknowledging that you are, in essence, a spiritual being affect the way you see yourself and the way you set priorities for your life?

+ What do you think it means to worship God "in spirit and truth" (John 4:24)?

SATAN DECLARES WAR

Introduction

God created human beings in His image and likeness so they could reflect His nature on earth and have close daily fellowship with Him. They were His beloved creation and were meant to worship Him *"in spirit and truth"* (John 4:24). Tragically, this wonderful fellowship and worship were disrupted. Why? The first human beings believed a lie from God's enemy, Satan, and broke trust with God. As a result, they brought on themselves and every other human being both a corrupt spiritual nature and inevitable physical death. Yet God did not allow that to be the end of the story for humanity. As we will see, He delivered us from Satan's power through His Son Jesus Christ and welcomed us back into His kingdom as His children and joint heirs with Jesus.

Memory Verse:

> *The god of this world [Satan] hath blinded the minds of them which believe not, lest the light of the glorious gospel of Christ, who is the image of God, should shine unto them.*
>
> (2 Corinthians 4:4 KJV)

Study Questions

1. How did God describe all of His earthly creation? (Genesis 1:31)

2. What do we read in the Bible that indicates God regularly had fellowship with human beings after creating them? (Genesis 3:8–9)

_____

_____

3. List three major roles that God gave to human beings on earth. (Genesis 1:26, 28)

(1) _____

(2) _____

(3) _____

4. What did God tell the first man, Adam, that he could *not* do? (Genesis 2:16–17a)

_____

5. What would happen if Adam did this thing? (Genesis 2:17b)

_____

6. What reason did the serpent give to encourage Adam's wife, Eve, to disobey this command from God? (Genesis 3:1–5)

_____

_____

7. In what ways were Adam and Eve already like God? (Genesis 1:26)

(1) _____

(2) _____

8. How did Adam and Eve respond to the serpent's temptation? (Genesis 3:6)

_____

9. What were the results for Adam and Eve—and the whole human race—due to their disobedience to God's command? (Romans 5:12; Genesis 3:16–19, 22–23)

_____

_____

_____

_____

10. Was the serpent's declaration that Adam and Eve would *not* die if they ate of the fruit of knowledge of good and evil a true statement? Why? (Genesis 3:19; 5:5)

_____

11. What is something all human beings have in common? (Romans 3:23)

_____

12. Besides the inevitability of physical death, what is another way in which human beings experience death? (Ephesians 2:1b)

_____

13. Name the identity of the serpent who tempted Adam and Eve. (Revelation 12:9; 20:2)

_____

14. Give the former name of this spiritual being and what this name signifies about his original nature. (Isaiah 14:12)

_____

15. What type of being was Lucifer (Satan, or the devil) previously? (Ezekiel 28:14–15)

_____

_____

16. What motivated Lucifer to become wicked and want to usurp God's reign? (Isaiah 14:13–14; Ezekiel 28:17; 1 Timothy 3:6)

_____

_____

17. List several terms Jesus used for Satan that reveal his present character. (Matthew 6:13; 13:19, 38; John 8:44; 10:10)

_____

_____

18. What title did Jesus use for Satan that indicates human beings relinquished their God-given rulership over the earth when they followed the serpent's suggestion instead of obeying God? (John 12:31; 14:30; 16:11)

_____

19. Besides human beings, what else was put into bondage when Adam and Eve disobeyed God? (Romans 8:20–21)

_____

20. Is Satan answerable to God? (Job 1:9–12; 2:6; John 16:11; Revelation 12:7–10)

_____

21. Though Satan usurped rule over the earth, who is always the world's ultimate Owner and Ruler? (Genesis 14:22; Matthew 11:25)

_____

22. What does the first chapter of the book of Job, as well as Jesus' words to His disciples in Matthew 16:19, show us about the relationship between the spiritual and physical worlds?

_____

_____

23. What is a major way in which Satan continues to deceive people? (2 Corinthians 11:13–15)

_____

_____

24. Besides various human beings, whom does Satan enlist to help carry out his wicked activities on earth? (Matthew 8:16; 12:22–28; 1 Timothy 4:1; Ephesians 6:12)

_____

_____

25. What is the origin of demons, or evil spirits? (Revelation 12:3–4a, 7–9; Jude 1:6; 2 Peter 2:4)

_____

26. List some of the evil things Satan is responsible for on earth. (Luke 13:10–16; Mark 9:16–27; Matthew 4:24; 13:18–19, 24–30, 36–42; Acts 10:38; 1 Chronicles 21:1–4; Luke 22:3–6; Acts 5:3; Ephesians 6:11 (NKJV, NIV); 2 Timothy 2:26; Hebrews 2:14–15; Revelation 2:10; 12:12)

_____

_____

_____

_____

27. What will God do on our behalf, as He did for the apostle Paul? (2 Timothy 4:18)

_____

28. Does God still desire daily fellowship with those whom He created in His image? (John 14:23; 1 John 1:3)

_____

For Further Reflection

+ How alert are you to potential deception and attacks from Satan in your life? In what ways can you be vigilant in this regard?

+ Do you regularly seek fellowship with God through prayer and reading the Bible? If not, how do you respond to Matthew 22:37?

Renewed by the Spirit

Introduction

Since all of humanity inherited a sinful nature and spiritual death, how can we have unbroken fellowship with God again, as He originally planned and still desires, and how can we fulfill His purposes for us? Our sinful nature separates us from God, who is holy*. The human spirit, made in the image and likeness of God, has been corrupted, making us even more vulnerable to Satan and his attacks. Sometimes, it has even made people the enemy's willing accomplices.

The answer that God has provided is forgiveness of our sins through His Son Jesus Christ; a renewed human spirit; and the sending of His own Holy Spirit to live within us. Having God's Spirit inside us means that we can now be fully on His side in this spiritual war and can live in agreement with His purposes. The *only* way to effectively engage in spiritual warfare is to be redeemed from our corrupt nature and to have a restored relationship with God, through which we are enabled to walk according to His Spirit. Then, we can put Satan's fallen angels under the feet of Jesus Christ in His name and through His shed blood. "*For [Jesus] must reign till He has put all enemies under His feet*" (1 Corinthians 15:25).

Memory Passage:

According to His mercy [God] saved us, through the washing of regeneration and renewing of the Holy Spirit, whom He poured out on us abundantly through Jesus Christ our Savior.

(Titus 3:5–6)

Study Questions

1. After the first human beings disobeyed God, what kind of nature did humanity have? (Ephesians 2:1b, 3; Romans 3:10–11, 23)

_____

_____

_____

2. Describe what is in control of those who have the above nature. (Romans 7:14, 18; 1 John 5:19)

_____

3. The Scriptures refer to following our own way rather than God's way as doing the *works of the flesh.* What are some of the works of the flesh*? (Galatians 5:19–21 NIV)

_____

_____

4. What has God provided to free us from the condition of being spiritually dead? (Colossians 2:13–14; John 3:16)

_____

_____

5. How do we apply God's provision through Christ to our own lives, so that we can be saved and reconciled to Him? (Romans 10:9)

_____

6. What did Jesus' death and resurrection free us from? (Hebrews 2:14–15; Colossians 1:13–14)

_____

_____

7. What is the result of our being in Christ? (2 Corinthians 5:17; Romans 6:5–7)

_____

_____

8. Are salvation and freedom from sin possible through anyone but Jesus Christ? (Acts 4:10, 12; John 3:13–16; 14:6; Matthew 24:4–5)

_____

9. What Spirit did we receive when our spirits were renewed in Christ? What are some of the attributes of this Spirit? (Acts 2:38; John 14:16–17; Romans 8:9, 15)

_____

_____

10. What does this Spirit give us? (John 6:63; Romans 8:10b)

_____

11. (a) Does our spiritual renewal also mean an immediate renewal of our physical bodies? (Romans 8:10)

_____

(b) What promise do we have regarding our physical bodies? (Romans 8:11; 1 Corinthians 15:50–55)

_____

12. What does God become to us when we are forgiven and receive His Spirit? (Romans 8:15b; Galatians 4:6)

_____

13. What do we become to God? (John 1:12–13; Romans 8:16–17; Galatians 4:7)

_____

14. As God's children, what are we now enabled to do, and what do we now have access to? (Hebrews 4:16; 10:19–22)

_____

15. Being renewed in our spirits does not mean we will never sin or struggle with wrong attitudes or thoughts anymore, since, while we are on this earth, we will still battle against the remnants of our sinful nature, as well as against Satan and his schemes, until Jesus returns to earth or we go to be with Him. What struggle between living by the Spirit and living by the old nature does the apostle Paul describe? (Romans 7:14–25)

_____

_____

16. There is a difference between our physical bodies, which we often call our "flesh" or "flesh and blood," and *the works of the flesh*, the fallen nature discussed in Galatians 5:19–21 and Romans 8:13. What three major areas of the fallen nature do we contend with? (1 John 2:16)

(1) _____

(2) _____

(3) _____

17. Satan often uses the *"lusts of our flesh ["sinful nature" NIV]"* (Ephesians 2:3) as a means of manipulating us. He tries to make his voice the prevailing influence in our lives, instead of God's voice, and to keep us from doing God's will. How can we overcome his attacks in this way? (Romans 8:1–6, 13–14; Galatians 5:16–17)

_____

_____

_____

18. What is the fruit (nature) of the Spirit, by which we are to live? (Galatians 5:22–23)

_____

_____

19. What is God able to do in order to strengthen us spiritually, according to the riches of His glory? (Ephesians 3:16–20)

_____

_____

_____

20. What important work does the Holy Spirit do in relation to our salvation and growth in faith? (2 Thessalonians 2:13b)

_____

21. How do we cooperate in the process of sanctification*? (Romans 12:1–2;
     Ephesians 4:22–24; Colossians 3:1–2, 5, 8–10)

_____

_____

_____

_____

_____

22. How can we know God and His ways? (1 Corinthians 2:12–14)

_____

_____

23. How can we renew our minds to conform to God's ways? (Hebrews 4:12;
     Psalm 19:7–14)

_____

_____

24. (a) What did Paul call the state of being carnally minded? (Romans 8:6a)

_____

     (b) What is the key to having true life and peace? (Romans 8:6b)

_____

25. What should we do if we sin, so that we can return to a right relationship with God? (1 John 1:9; 2:1–2)

_____

26. (a) Once we have been reconciled to God through Christ, what ministry has He given us? (2 Corinthians 5:18)

_____

(b) What is the message of this ministry? Complete the following:

2 Corinthians 5:19: "*That God was in* _____ *reconciling the*

_____ *to Himself, not imputing their* _____ *to them.*"

(c) What term did Paul use for those engaged in this ministry? (Verse 20a)

_____

For Further Reflection

+ Being honest with yourself, would you describe yourself as mainly "*carnally minded*" or "*spiritually minded*" (Romans 8:6)? What have you learned in this study about how you can overcome the fleshly (carnal) nature and become spiritually minded?

+ Isaiah 55:6 says, "*Seek the* Lord *while He may be found, call upon Him while He is near.*" Have you been putting off salvation, thinking that you can be saved "tomorrow"? Do not let Satan deceive you into believing you can live your life any way you want, without a true relationship with God, and then come to Him whenever you feel like it. Don't wait until it's too late. Be reconciled to God and become a new creation in Christ. I invite you to pray this prayer:

> Heavenly Father, I come to You in the name of Your Son Jesus. I believe that You sent Him to earth to die for my sins and that You raised Him from the dead so that I might be completely forgiven and righteous in Him. I ask Jesus Christ to come into my heart and to save my soul, so that my sins may be washed away by the blood of the Lamb. Thank You for accepting me through Jesus, giving me eternal life, and welcoming me into Your family as Your own child. In Jesus' name, amen.

Study 4

WHAT SPIRITUAL WARFARE IS ALL ABOUT

Introduction

Once they have been saved and have received the Holy Spirit, some people think that their lives will be free of all problems. We must realize that being restored to God doesn't remove us from spiritual warfare; it doesn't mean we will never be attacked by the enemy again. The devil not only wants to thwart our ministry as ambassadors of reconciliation who bring the gospel of salvation to other people, but he also wants to destroy us—in this life and for eternity. The love, forgiveness, and grace of God are in complete contrast to the utter wickedness of Satan, who endeavors to change our allegiance back to him. If he can't do that, he tries to sidetrack us by making us feel defeated or by diverting us in other ways, so that we are ineffective in our faith. Remember that he desires to deceive and torment people. Some of the difficulties we encounter in our lives are manifestations of the spiritual battle that is taking place right now in the invisible spiritual realm.

Yet, because we have been reconciled to God and are now His children, we have the ability to fight back against Satan. We do not need to be oppressed and victimized by him any longer! We can actively enter the spiritual battle in the power of God's Spirit and live in the victory over the enemy that Jesus has already achieved for us through His death and resurrection.

Memory Passage:

For we do not wrestle against flesh and blood, but against principalities, against powers, against the rulers of the darkness of this age, against spiritual hosts of wickedness in the heavenly places.
(Ephesians 6:12)

Study Questions

1. What two distinct realms are involved in spiritual warfare? (Matthew 12:25–28; Colossians 1:13 NKJV, NIV)

(1) _____ (2) _____

2. What are some major differences between these realms? (3 John 1:11; John 10:10; Luke 13:10–16)

_____

_____

_____

3. As a review from study 1, list several aspects of God's nature. (Leviticus 19:2; 1 John 4:8, 16; Romans 1:20)

_____

_____

4. Name three major characteristics of God's kingdom, which all come through the Holy Spirit. (Romans 14:17)

(1) _____ (2) _____ (3) _____

5. As a review from previous studies, list several depictions of Satan that reveal his nature. (John 8:44; 10:10; Matthew 13:19; Revelation 12:9)

_____

_____

6. List some designations for Satan's kingdom. (Colossians 1:13; Ephesians 6:12)

_____

_____

7. Read Isaiah's vision of God on His heavenly throne and the apostle John's vision of Jesus Christ in heaven. What do these descriptions tell us about God? (Isaiah 6:1–8; Revelation 1:12–17)

_____

8. What three things did Satan try to tempt Jesus Christ to do? (Matthew 4:1–10)

(1) _____

(2) _____

(3) _____

9. What does Satan (*"the dragon"*) want all peoples on earth to do? (Revelation 13:4, 8, 11–15)

_____

10. What are the major methods the devil uses to draw people away from God? (Genesis 3:1–6, 13; 2 Corinthians 4:4; Revelation 20:3)

_____

11. When human beings turn away from God, what does this do to the image and likeness of God in which they were created? (Romans 1:28–32)

_____

_____

_____

_____

12. How can we can manifest the nature of God and continue in His ways? (1 John 2:26–28; John 15:4–5)

_____

_____

13. What is Satan called in relation to those who have put their faith in Christ? (Revelation 12:10)

_____

14. How can we protect ourselves against Satan's accusations? (Romans 8:1; 1 John 2:1–2)

_____

_____

_____

15. What did Jesus do to the principalities and powers of the kingdom of darkness when He redeemed us through His death on the cross? (Colossians 2:15)

_____

16. What types of power and authority over the devil does Jesus give believers? (Luke 9:1–2; 10:19)

_____

_____

17. Which kingdom and which nature—the kingdom of God or the kingdom of darkness—will prevail in the end? (Matthew 16:18; 1 Corinthians 15:24–25; Revelation 11:15–17)

_____

18. How do we know that the devil has already been defeated in his plan to overthrow God's kingdom? (Revelation 12:7–11; 20:2–3, 10; Hebrews 2:14; Colossians 2:15)

_____

_____

_____

19. On whom should we always rely for our victory over the enemy? (Romans 5:17; 1 Corinthians 15:57; 2 Corinthians 2:14)

_____

20. As we live out our faith and experience testings and trials, including spiritual warfare, what can we count on to make us *more than conquerors*? (Romans 8:35–39)

_____

_____

21. (a) What will God do for us, and what has He already done, to keep us in Him? Complete the following:

2 Corinthians 1:21–22: *"Now He who _____ us with*

you in Christ and _____ us is God, who also has

_____ us and _____ _____

_____ in our hearts as a guarantee."

(b) What did Paul pray God would do for the Thessalonian believers to safeguard them for the day when Christ would return? Complete the following:

1 Thessalonians 5:23: *"May the God of peace Himself _____ you*

completely; and may your whole spirit, soul, and body be _____

_____ at the coming of our Lord Jesus Christ."

(c) What assurance of the above did Paul give? (Verse 24)

_____

22. What did Jesus promise to do to sustain and strengthen us until spiritual warfare is ended? (Matthew 28:20b)

_____

For Further Reflection

+ Satan desires to accuse us of sin and failure in order to discourage us. In what ways have you experienced his accusations against you because of past or present sins? How will you respond to them according to Romans 8:1 and 1 John 2:1–2?

+ Are the characteristics of God's kingdom—righteousness, peace, and joy—evident in your life? Why or why not? If you are not generally experiencing these aspects of the kingdom, meditate on the following Scriptures every day: 2 Corinthians 5:21; John 14:27; 1 Peter 4:12–13.

PART II
A GLOBAL WAR/A PERSONAL WAR

Enlisted in God's Army

Introduction

Spiritual warfare can be considered a war that Satan wages against the whole world—a global war. The apostle John wrote, *"We know that we are of God, and the whole world lies under the sway of the wicked one"* (1 John 5:19). Satan wants to gather the kingdoms of the world against God in a final battle to overthrow Him. (See, for example, Revelation 16:14.) Yet spiritual warfare can also be considered a war Satan conducts against individuals—a personal war. For example, Satan made focused attacks on Job (see, for example, Job 1:1–12), and he specifically asked God if he could *"sift"* Peter (see Luke 22:31–32).

As a child of God and a joint heir with Jesus Christ, you have been given spiritual authority, and you are enlisted in God's army to fight against and overcome the works of the devil—whether they are attacks against multitudes or individuals, including yourself. The enemy doesn't want you to know that you have this authority to defeat him. Yet your effectiveness against his evil power, and your deliverance from his attacks, can be taken away only if you relinquish the spiritual rights and responsibilities you have received in Christ. In this study, we will learn more about those rights and responsibilities so that we can live them out and experience victory in spiritual warfare.

Memory Verse:

Be strong in the Lord and in the power of His might.   （Ephesians 6:10)

Study Questions

1. What did the apostle Paul tell Timothy he must do and be? (2 Timothy 2:3)

    _____

2. What are some ways Jesus expects His followers to engage in spiritual warfare? (Matthew 10:8; Luke 10:1, 17–19)

    _____

    _____

3. Give some important reasons why we should participate in spiritual warfare. (Matthew 10:8b; Mark 9:38–40; John 14:12–15)

    _____

    _____

    _____

4. What are some keys to remember when we are waging warfare against the enemy? (1 Corinthians 16:13–14; Galatians 5:1)

    _____

5. What point was the apostle Paul making in 2 Timothy 2:4–5?

    _____

6. Summarize how we should we live and work alongside other believers as we engage in spiritual warfare. (Philippians 1:27–28; 2:1–4, 14–16)

_____

_____

_____

_____

_____

7. What are some ways by which God equips us to fulfill His purposes? (John 14:16–17; Philippians 2:13; Hebrews 13:20–21)

_____

_____

_____

8. Who is stronger: Satan or the typical human being? (1 John 5:19b)

_____

9. Who is stronger: Satan or the human being who has been redeemed? (1 John 4:4)

_____

10. What general steps are we instructed to take in order to fend off the devil? (James 4:7)

(1) _____

(2) _____

11. What is the nature of the "weapons" we are to use in spiritual warfare? (2 Corinthians 10:4)

_____

_____

12. List some specific aspects of the spiritual armor Paul instructed us to put on and use. (Ephesians 6:14–17)

_____

_____

13. What portion of the spiritual armor that God has given us are we to use? (Ephesians 6:11, 13)

_____

14. Who should receive credit for the victory in the spiritual battles we fight? (1 Samuel 17:47; Zechariah 4:6b)

_____

15. Hebrews 11 mentions specific people in the Old Testament who were commended for their faith in God. Some were faithful witnesses to the point of death, while others were miraculously delivered, according to God's purposes. List some remarkable works that God's people did through their faith in Him. (Hebrews 11:32–34)

_____

_____

_____

16. Where does our strength against the enemy come from? (Ephesians 6:10; Philippians 4:13)

_____

_____

17. How did the believers mentioned in the book of Revelation overcome Satan? (Revelation 12:11)

(1) _____

(2) _____

(3) _____

18. What is the Lord* faithful to do for us in relation to the devil (*"the evil one"*)? (2 Thessalonians 3:3)

(1) _____ (2) _____

For Further Reflection

- Have you thought of Satan as being stronger than you are, even though Christ lives within you and is infinitely greater than the enemy? If so, repeat 1 John 4:4 and Ephesians 6:10 when you become discouraged or afraid.

- In James 4:7, we are instructed to submit to God and resist the devil. Can you resist the devil without first submitting to God? Why? Are you submitting to God in your life?

- What do you think it means to *draw near to God,* based on James 4:8?

The Stakes Are High

Introduction

We have seen that we were created to love God, to worship Him, and to live for Him. When we are reconciled to God the Father through His Son Jesus Christ, we are able to fulfill these purposes as we reach out to others so that they, too, may be reconciled to Him and receive all the blessings He desires to give them. Yet Satan wants to destroy every person on earth, in whatever ways he can. The "stakes" in spiritual warfare are the highest—they involve both the state of people's lives on earth and their eternal destinies.

The wonderful news is that the mercy of God has provided healing and deliverance from the spiritual forces of darkness through Jesus Christ. Matthew 4:16 says, "*The people who sat in darkness have seen a great light, and upon those who sat in the region and shadow of death Light has dawned.*" Although we live in a day of great trouble and spiritual deception, we also have a great Deliverer who frees the captives! Let us acknowledge what is at stake for us and others as we work alongside God to free those whom the enemy has taken captive and oppressed.

Memory Verse:

The Spirit of the Lord is upon Me, because He has anointed Me to preach the gospel to the poor; He has sent Me to heal the brokenhearted, to proclaim liberty to the captives and recovery of sight to the blind, to set at liberty those who are oppressed. (Luke 4:18)

Study Questions

1. What terms did (1) Jesus and (2) the apostle Paul use for Satan in relation to this present world? (John 12:31b; 2 Corinthians 4:4a)

(1) _____ (2) _____

2. What influence has the world generally been under since the fall of humanity? (1 John 5:19b)

_____

3. How is the present age characterized? (Galatians 1:4)

_____

4. What did Satan come to do on the earth? (John 10:10a)

(1) _____ (2) _____ (3) _____

5. For what purpose did Jesus come to earth? (John 3:17; 10:10b; 1 John 3:8b)

_____

6. Every person will end up with one of two eternal destinies. Name them, below. (Daniel 12:2; John 3:16–18; 5:25–29)

(1) _____

(2) _____

7. Will anyone be exempt from judgment for his "works," or actions, on earth? (Revelation 20:11–13)

_____

8. Who will be condemned at the end of the age? (Joel 3:12–14; Revelation 20:14–15)

_____

_____

9. Even though Satan is temporarily allowed to work his darkness on the earth, who ultimately rules over the nations of the world? (2 Chronicles 20:6)

_____

10. List three aspects of God's ultimate plan for the earth. (Habakkuk 2:14; Luke 11:2b; Revelation 11:15b)

(1) _____

(2) _____

(3) _____

11. (a) What is God's attitude toward those who are currently living under the power of the devil and according to the sinful nature? (Mark 2:17; 2 Peter 3:9)

_____

(b) What does God want to do for those who are in jeopardy of eternal death? (Zechariah 3:1–5)

_____

12. Before we were saved through faith in Christ, what did we live according to, and what were we by nature? (Ephesians 2:1b–3)

_____

_____

_____

13. What did God do for us in His mercy and love? (Ephesians 2:1a, 4–8)

_____

_____

_____

14. What does Satan do to human beings through his demons? (Mark 9:14–22; Luke 8:26–29)

_____

15. What did demons recognize about Jesus? (Luke 4:33–34; 8:28, 31)

_____

_____

16. What did demons recognize about themselves when confronted by Jesus? (Matthew 8:29)

_____

17. List various aspects of Jesus' stated mission on the earth. (John 10:10; Luke 4:18; 19:10)

_____

_____

_____

_____

18. Give some examples of how Jesus fulfilled His mission. (Matthew 8:16–17; 11:4–5; Luke 19:1–9)

_____

_____

19. To whom did Jesus entrust the continuation of this mission? (Luke 9:1–6; 10:1; Mark 16:14–18)

_____

_____

20. How did the disciples and other believers carry on Jesus' mission after He returned to God the Father in heaven? (Mark 16:19–20; Acts 2:1–41, 43, 47b; 3:1–10; 5:12–16; 8:25–40; 16:16–18)

_____

_____

_____

21. Whom did Jesus say were His disciples? (John 8:31; 13:35; 15:7–9; Matthew 7:21–23)

_____

_____

22. What should we be doing today as disciples of Jesus? (John 14:15; Ephesians 2:10; Matthew 9:35–38; John 14:12)

_____

_____

_____

23. What assurances do we have that God will keep us safe in Him as we continue Jesus' mission in the world? (John 17:11, 15–20; Jude 1:24)

_____

_____

For Further Reflection

- Do you share God's attitude toward the lost and oppressed? Ask Him to give you His heart of compassion and commitment toward those who are still under the power of the devil and need to receive Jesus as Savior and Lord*, be healed, or be delivered.

- Whom do you know who needs to be sought out and saved, as Jesus sought out Zacchaeus? Pray daily for that person.

- Pray that the Lord of the harvest will send out laborers into His "field," the world.

- What are you doing as a disciple of Jesus Christ today?

Satan's Strategies and Attacks, Part 1

Introduction

Satan uses various schemes and methods to keep people from coming to know and love God, and to prevent those who do know and love Him from living out their faith effectively and thereby defeating his strategies. The devil may attack us directly, or he may try to tempt our sinful "flesh*" to disobey God. I have seen Christians become discouraged, lose hope, and even forsake their faith because of tests, temptations, and trials. This alarms me because, in visions and revelations, I have seen the cruel hate the enemy has for humanity, and I have seen the fate of those who die without the Lord*. We need to understand and apply the deliverance God has provided for us!

To do this, we must be aware of the strategies Satan uses against us. In this study, after several questions to set the stage, we will begin to investigate seven major areas through which Satan may attack us directly or fuel the fire under our fleshly desires, and how we can counteract these assaults of the devil and the carnal nature. As we do, we will expand on some of the topics we began to look at in earlier studies, as well as explore new areas related to spiritual warfare. We must take dominion and authority over the demons that Satan sends against us and our loved ones—such as demons of anger, depression, and suicide—and put them under Jesus' feet, so that we can be free to serve the Lord with joy.

Memory Passage:

Be sober, be vigilant; because your adversary the devil walks about like a roaring lion, seeking whom he may devour. Resist him, steadfast in the faith, knowing that the same sufferings are experienced by your brotherhood [fellow believers] in the world. (1 Peter 5:8–9)

Study Questions

1. Even as Satan wages warfare against God, he is still under God's authority. What is he sometimes referred to as, and what can we infer from this name about the realm he is temporarily allowed to act within? (Ephesians 2:2)

   _____

   _____

2. List the names of various evil entities that Satan uses to carry out his works of darkness—entities that we battle against. (Ephesians 6:12)

   (1) _____ (2) _____

   (3) _____

   (4) _____

3. What are Satan's various strategies against human beings called in Ephesians 6:11 in the following Bible translations?

   New King James Version: _____

   New International Version: _____

4. What should our general approach be to protecting ourselves from Satan's strategies and attacks? (1 Peter 5:8–9)

   _____

   _____

Satanic Strategy 1: Deceit

5. What disguise does the devil use in order to mislead people and prompt them to think and do what he wants? (2 Corinthians 11:14)

_____

6. Satan incited Eve to sin by getting her to doubt God's Word (see Genesis 3:1–6), a strategy he continues to use frequently on human beings. Give two reasons why he is so determined to undermine our faith in God's Word.

(1) Mark 11:23: _____

_____

(2) Romans 14:23b:_____

_____

7. What are some truths we can stand on to counteract Satan's attempts to make us doubt God's Word? (Psalm 119:160; John 1:1, 4, 9, 17; 1 Thessalonians 2:13; Hebrews 11:6b)

_____

_____

_____

8. What are some other ways in which Satan tries to deceive people? (Matthew 7:15; 1 Timothy 4:1–2; 2 Timothy 2:25–26; 2 Corinthians 4:3–4)

_____

9. How are we instructed to counteract this type of deception?

1 John 4:1: _____

_____

Matthew 7:16–20: _____

_____

10. What did Paul say would happen when believers became unified in their faith and in their knowledge of Jesus and attained *the measure of the stature of the fullness of Christ* (Ephesians 4:13)? (Verse 14)

_____

_____

11. One form of false doctrine is to quote God's Word out of context, thereby twisting its meaning. What did Jesus do when Satan tried to use this tactic on Him? (Matthew 4:1–11)

_____

_____

12. Name an additional method by which Satan deceives by imitating the works of God. (Mark 13:22; 2 Thessalonians 2:8–10)

_____

13. How can we recognize false signs and wonders and therefore keep from being deceived by this method? (Matthew 7:16–23; John 17:3)

_____

_____

_____

Satanic Strategy 2: Temptation

14. (a) Does God ever tempt people? (James 1:13)

_____

(b) What causes us to be tempted? (Verse 14)

_____

(c) When an ungodly desire is "conceived," what does it give birth to? (Verse 15a)

_____

(d) When sin is fully grown, what does it give birth to? (Verse 15b)

_____

15. List various sinful practices that we can be tempted to engage in, either by our own fleshly nature or by Satan's enticements. (Proverbs 28:7; Romans 13:13; 1 John 2:16; Ephesians 2:3; 1 Timothy 3:3; 6:9–10; 1 Peter 4:3)

_____

_____

_____

16. In what way can lusts of the flesh* tragically lead people to succumb to false teaching? (2 Peter 2:12–22)

_____

_____

_____

17. What assurances do we have from God's Word that we can overcome temptation? (1 Corinthians 10:13; James 4:7)

_____

_____

_____

18. What encouragement can we draw from Jesus' life in relation to temptation? (Matthew 4:1–11; Hebrews 4:14–16)

_____

_____

_____

19. Because Jesus defeated the devil's temptations in the wilderness, did this mean He was never tempted by the devil again? (Luke 4:13)

_____

20. List various ways by which we can equip ourselves to resist temptation.
    (Mark 14:38; Galatians 5:16, 24; Romans 6:12; 8:13–14; 13:14; Ephesians 4:22–24;
    1 Thessalonians 4:3–5; 1 Timothy 6:6–8, 11; Colossians 3:1–2; Philippians 4:8)

_____

_____

_____

_____

_____

_____

_____

21. What warning and promise do we find in Galatians 6:8?

_____

_____

Satanic Strategy 3: Accusation/Condemnation

22. Remember that Satan is called *"the accuser of our brethren"* (Revelation 12:10), and one of his strategies involves making us feel guilty for sins and failures and causing us to doubt God's forgiveness. Name some ways in which we leave ourselves open to the devil's accusations and condemnation. (Luke 22:54–62; Romans 7:14–15; 1 Timothy 3:7)

_____

_____

_____

23. How are we to respond when we have sinned? (1 John 1:9; Matthew 5:23–24; James 5:16a; Hebrews 12:1)

_____

_____

_____

24. While Satan accuses us and tries to make us feel guilty when we sin, God's approach is to convict us and to discipline us, so that we may become more like Him. (See Hebrews 12:5–8 NKJV, NIV.) Why does God take this approach? Complete the following:

    Hebrews 12:6a: *"For whom the* LORD _____ *He chastens."*

25. What do the following verses say about our identity and relationship to God once we have confessed our sins and repented?

Romans 8:1: _____

_____

2 Corinthians 5:17a, 18a: _____

_____

For Further Reflection

+ Have you lived in fear of Satan and his attacks? Meditate on such Scriptures as Deuteronomy 33:27 and Romans 8:35–39.

+ What type of temptation are you most likely to yield to? Why? Using Jesus' example of answering temptation by the Word of God, what Scriptures directly address your temptation? Reviewing the ways in which you can defeat temptation listed in question 19, above, which responses seem most applicable to your situation?

Satan's Strategies and Attacks, Part 2

Introduction

Those who truly believe God and are earnestly following Christ often face trials that are much more demanding than those other people experience, because demonic spirits are generally sent out on various assignments against us based on our spiritual strength and usefulness in Christ. In such circumstances, one difficulty seems to follow another, since it is the strategy of these demonic forces to weigh us down with so much trouble at once that we relinquish our confession of faith, temporarily—or permanently.

In this study, we will continue to explore Satan's strategies and attacks so that we can recognize them and conquer them. As we do, please keep in mind that various Scripture passages that are presented for overcoming the enemy in regard to one of his strategies may also be appropriate in regard to another of his strategies. You should apply Scriptures to your life wherever they are relevant. In all cases, for us to wage effective warfare, we must first bind the "strong man," which is what Jesus called Satan. (See Matthew 12:29.) The enemy and his demon powers must be put under the feet of Jesus Christ in His name and through His blood. As the Scriptures say, *"For this purpose the Son of God was manifested, that He might destroy the works of the devil"* (1 John 3:8).

Memory Verse:

And I will give you the keys of the kingdom of heaven, and whatever you bind on earth will be bound in heaven, and whatever you loose on earth will be loosed in heaven.

(Matthew 16:19)

Study Questions

Satanic Strategy 4: Preying on Spiritual Vulnerability

26. What did the apostle Paul say to warn believers about allowing the devil to influence their lives, which would leave them spiritually vulnerable to his attacks and deception? (Ephesians 4:26–27 NKJV, NIV)

_____

_____

27. Name some other ways in which people may allow Satan access to their lives. (Deuteronomy 1:26–32; 1 Samuel 15:23; Matthew 6:14–15; Hebrews 12:15; 1 Timothy 5:22; Psalm 73:2–3; Revelation 3:16–17)

_____

_____

_____

_____

_____

_____

28. What are some major ways in which we can protect ourselves from being spiritually vulnerable? (Mark 11:24–25; Proverbs 3:5–6; 2 Timothy 1:7)

_____

_____

_____

_____

Satanic Strategy 5: Provoking People to Sin

29. Read the Scripture passages describing the situations of the following people in the Old and New Testaments whom Satan wanted to provoke to sin—sometimes successfully. Then, answer the questions relating to each circumstance.

   Job: (Job 1:1–19; 2:1–9) Satan claimed that Job served God only because he was blessed by Him and that Job would curse God to His face if everything he loved and owned was taken away from him, and if he was attacked in his body with terrible illness. God allowed Satan to inflict these things on Job, but Job did not take Satan's bait. Although Job eventually repented of presumption after coming to know God in a deeper way through his calamitous experiences (see Job 42:5–7), what kept him from sinning when Satan attacked him? (Job 1:20–22; 2:10; 13:15a)

_____

_____

David: (1 Chronicles 21:1–7) David was incited by Satan to count the number of fighting men he had available so he would feel secure in his military strength. His general, Joab, objected. Yet David numbered them anyway, and God was displeased with him. Why was David's action sinful? (Verse 3; see also Judges 7.)

_____

_____

_____

_____

Judas Iscariot: (Luke 22:1–6, 47–53; John 13:2) Satan incited Judas by "entering him" or "putting it into his heart" to betray Jesus to the authorities who were trying to kill Him, and Judas did so. Jesus referred to Judas as *the son of perdition* who would be spiritually lost for betraying Him. What led Judas to this dire spiritual state? (Matthew 26:6–15; John 6:70–71; 12:1–6; 17:12; Acts 1:24–25)

_____

_____

_____

Ananias and Sapphira: (Acts 5:1–11) This couple in the early church saw other believers selling land and giving all the money to the apostles. They apparently wanted people to praise them for taking similar action, and Satan "filled their hearts" or incited them to pretend to give all the proceeds from the sale of their land but actually keep some of the profits. The apostle Peter discerned by the Holy Spirit that they were lying about the proceeds, pointing out that they could have done anything they wanted with their own money and didn't need to claim to have given it all. Why did they come to such a disastrous end? (Verses 4b, 9a, 11)

_____

_____

30. (a) Which "member" of the body did the apostle James say can be *"set on fire by hell,"* or incited by Satan and his demons? (James 3:6)

_____

(b) Describe this "member" by completing the following:

James 3:6: *"The* _____ *is a fire, a* _____ _____

_____. *The tongue is so set among our members that it*

_____ _____ _____ _____, *and*

sets on fire _____ _____ _____ _____*."*

(c) How can we extinguish those flames, or keep them from igniting in the first place? (James 1:19–20; Ephesians 4:29; Psalm 4:4–5)

_____

_____

31. What are some other ways we can resist being incited to sin by Satan? (1 Corinthians 13; 1 Thessalonians 5:16–18)

_____

_____

Satanic Strategy 6: Invasive Force

32. We have previously established that Satan's demons sometimes invade people's bodies and possess them—in certain cases, to the point of controlling their words and actions. (See, for example, Luke 8:26–29.)

    (a) What is another invasive method Satan uses against people? (Luke 8:11–12)

    _____

    (b) How can they prevent him from succeeding? (Verse 15)

    _____

    _____

33. Although not all physical affliction can be directly attributed to Satan, he sometimes does attack people in physical ways. How do the following biblical passages support this fact? (Luke 13:10–17; Acts 10:38)

    _____

    _____

34. (a) What did Jesus indicate must be done to the *strong man* (Satan) who invades people's lives? (Matthew 12:28–29)

    _____

    (b) What privilege and responsibility did Jesus give His followers in this regard? (Matthew 16:19; 18:18)

    _____

    _____

(c) When a person has been delivered from a demon, why is it essential that he receive Jesus Christ as Lord and Savior, be filled with the Holy Spirit, and walk according to the Spirit? (Luke 11:24–26)

_____

_____

_____

Satanic Strategy 7: Persecution

35. Read the following biblical passages that describe believers being persecuted for their faith, and then answer the question that follows: Luke 21:11–13, 16–17; Acts 7:57–8:3; 13:49–50; 26:10–11; Hebrews 11:35b–40; Daniel 7:21–22, 25–26; Revelation 2:8–11.

    Should we be surprised when we, also, are persecuted for our faith? Why or why not? (Mark 10:29–30; John 15:20; 2 Timothy 3:12)

_____

_____

36. In what way did Jesus describe those who are persecuted for their faith in Him, and what did He say they would receive? (Matthew 5:10–12)

_____

_____

37. (a) Why did the apostle Peter write that we ought to rejoice in persecution? (1 Peter 4:12–14)

_____

_____

_____

(b) What is a reason some people may suffer that is *not* persecution? (1 Peter 4:15)

_____

_____

38. What do some people do when they are persecuted? (Mark 4:16–17)

_____

39. In what ways should we respond to persecution? (Matthew 5:44; 10:16–19, 22; Romans 5:3–4; 12:14; 2 Corinthians 12:10; 2 Thessalonians 1:4; 1 Peter 4:19; Hebrews 12:11)

_____

_____

_____

_____

_____

_____

_____

_____

40. Read Luke 22:41–53. Why was Jesus persecuted to the point of crucifixion? (Luke 22:42, 53)

_____

_____

41. What positive outcomes does persecution sometimes result in? (Matthew 10:17–18; Acts 8:3–7)

_____

_____

42. What seven characteristics must we add to our faith in order to establish our calling to salvation and to God's purposes and keep from stumbling spiritually? (2 Peter 1:5–7)

(1) _____ (2) _____ (3) _____

(4) _____ (5) _____ (6) _____

(7) _____

43. Regardless of the persecution we may encounter, who will "confirm" us to the end, so that we may be blameless before God at the end of the age? (1 Corinthians 1:7b)

_____

For Further Reflection

+ In what way(s) might you be spiritually vulnerable for Satan to get a foothold in your life? How will you seal off this vulnerability, based on the study you just completed?

+ In what situation(s) do you need to "bind the strong man" to release someone from Satan's oppression? How will you proceed in doing this?

+ Are you experiencing persecution in some way? If so, bless and pray for those who are mistreating you and extend to them forgiveness and the compassion of Christ.

Part III

Enabling Our Warfare

THE HOLY SPIRIT: COMFORTER, HELPER, AND GUIDE

Introduction

In study 3, we talked about how the Holy Spirit indwells us, renews us, and keeps us strong in our faith. Let us now explore some additional ways in which the Spirit helps us as we engage in spiritual warfare. When we have the Holy Spirit living inside us, we have God's nature and power within, and we have access to His resources and weapons for warfare. Let's be sure to receive all aspects of the powerful support God wants to give us for the spiritual battles we undergo. "*The natural man does not receive the things of the Spirit of God, for they are foolishness to him; nor can he know them, because they are spiritually discerned*" (1 Corinthians 2:14). Pray that you may discern and avail yourself of the resources of the Spirit of God* for your life.

Memory Passage:

The Spirit also helps in our weaknesses. For we do not know what we should pray for as we ought, but the Spirit Himself makes intercession for us with groanings which cannot be uttered. Now He who searches the hearts knows what the mind of the Spirit is, because He makes intercession for the saints according to the will of God. (Romans 8:26–27)

Study Questions

1. Even though Jesus had already "*breathed*" the Holy Spirit on His followers after His resurrection (see John 20:22), what did He say would happen to them? (Acts 1:5b)

2. (a) What would His followers receive when this occurred? (Acts 1:8a)

_____

(b) What was the purpose of this bestowment? (Verse 8b)

_____

3. (a) What did the promised coming of the Holy Spirit sound like? (Acts 2:2)

_____

(b) What did it look like? (Verse 3)

_____

4. What happened when Jesus followers were filled, or "baptized," with the Holy Spirit? (Acts 2:4b)

_____

5. The baptism in the Holy Spirit gave Peter the power to witness about Jesus to the multitudes who had gathered in Jerusalem to celebrate Pentecost. How many people responded to the message of salvation? (Acts 2:41)

_____

6. What happened after the believers later prayed that God would enable them to speak His Word with great boldness, to heal, and to perform miraculous signs and wonders in the name of Jesus? (See Acts 4:29–30.)

Acts 4:31, 33a:

_____

_____

Acts 5:12a:

_____

7. (a) Similar to the experience of the original believers, what did the Samaritan believers still need to receive after having been baptized in water in the name of Jesus? (Acts 8:14–17)

_____

(b) How did Peter and John know that the Samaritans had not yet been baptized in the Holy Spirit? Complete the following:

Acts 8:16a: *"For as yet He had* _____ _____

_____ _____ _____.*"*

8. What did Jesus call the Holy Spirit in John 14:26, as translated in the following Bible versions?

New King James Version: _____

King James Version: _____

New International Version: _____

9. What did Jesus say the Holy Spirit would do for believers, in addition to giving them power? (John 14:26b)

_____

_____

10. When Jesus was on earth, He answered the devil's temptations with Scripture. (See Luke 4:1–12.) How is the Holy Spirit's role, as described in John 14:26, a help to us in spiritual warfare?

_____

_____

11. Name some additional ways in which the Spirit supports us. (John 16:13, 15; 1 Corinthians 2:12)

_____

_____

12. Complete the following: God's Spirit is the Spirit of… (Isaiah 11:2)

(1) _____ and _____

(2) _____ and _____

(3) _____

(4) _____

13. How does the Spirit help us when we do not know what to pray? (Romans 8:26b–27)

_____

_____

14. In what way has the Spirit of God* sometimes acted on or worked in people to fulfill His will? (Judges 13:25; Ezra 1:5; Haggai 1:14; Luke 2:25–32; Acts 18:5)

_____

_____

15. Name nine aspects of the fruit of the Spirit, which reflect facets of God's character that are to become increasingly evident in our lives. (Galatians 5:22–23)

(1) _____ (2) _____ (3) _____

(4) _____ (5) _____ (6) _____

(7) _____ (8) _____ (9) _____

16. Recall what Jesus said we should do, so that we may be "sons of our Father in heaven." (Matthew 5:44–45)

_____

_____

17. Read Romans 12:17–21. What statement sums up the way we are to overcome evil? (Verse 21b)

_____

18. In the following instances, explain how Jesus overcame evil in the above way:

Luke 22:47–51: _____

_____

Luke 23:33–34: _____

_____

19. How did Luke, the author of Acts, describe the believers in the early church? Complete the following:

Acts 9:31b: *"And walking in the* _____ _____ _____ _____

and in the _____ _____ _____ _____

_____, *they were* _____."

For Further Reflection

+ Is there a particular difficulty in your life for which there seems to be no solution? Commit the matter to God and ask the Holy Spirit to intercede on your behalf regarding it.

+ Daily ask the Holy Spirit to reveal His wisdom, understanding, counsel, might, knowledge, and fear of the Lord* to you and through you.

+ In what specific ways can you overcome evil with good this week? Which aspects of the fruit of the Spirit correspond with those ways?

Study 10

THE HOLY SPIRIT'S GIFTS

Introduction

In this lesson, we continue to learn the role of the Holy Spirit in spiritual warfare by looking more closely at the nine "gifts of the Spirit" listed in 1 Corinthians 12:7–10. We will also explore the way the Holy Spirit gives discernment, visions, and revelations to aid our spiritual understanding, enable God's work to be accomplished, and help us to battle the enemy. Again, we must seek to receive and exercise all the supernatural endowments the Lord* wants to give us.

Memory Passage:

> But the manifestation of the Spirit is given to each one for the profit of all: for to one is given the word of wisdom through the Spirit, to another the word of knowledge through the same Spirit, to another faith by the same Spirit, to another gifts of healings by the same Spirit, to another the working of miracles, to another prophecy, to another discerning of spirits, to another different kinds of tongues, to another the interpretation of tongues. But one and the same Spirit works all these things, distributing to each one individually as He wills.
>
> (1 Corinthians 12:7–11)

Study Questions

1. Name five "ministry gifts" that the Holy Spirit bestows on certain believers to enable them to exercise spiritual leadership in the church. (Ephesians 4:11–12) [continued, next page]

(1) _____ (2) _____

(3) _____ (4) _____

(5) _____

2. List the nine "gifts of the Spirit," distributed by the Holy Spirit to each believer as He wills, in order to build up the body of Christ and equip believers for spiritual warfare. (1 Corinthians 12:7–10)

(1) _____ (2) _____

(3) _____ (4) _____

(5) _____ (6) _____

(7) _____ (8) _____

(9) _____

3. Do all believers have the same spiritual gift(s)? Explain. (1 Corinthians 12:4–7, 11–12)

_____

_____

4. How has the Holy Spirit used the gifts of supernatural wisdom and supernatural knowledge to aid believers in doing God's will?

(a) Supernatural wisdom: (Acts 8:26–40)

_____

_____

(b) Supernatural knowledge: (Acts 16:6–12; 19:21)

_____

_____

_____

5. In addition to the special gifts of the word of wisdom and the word of knowledge, which are given to certain believers as the Spirit wills, how does the Holy Spirit help all believers through discernment and wisdom? (Isaiah 30:21; John 16:13; James 1:5–8)

_____

_____

6. What did Stephen do as a result of the gift of faith in his life? (Acts 6:8)

_____

7. Jesus operated in all the gifts of the Spirit. How were the gifts of healings evident in His ministry? (Matthew 4:23; 9:35)

_____

_____

8. How did Philip and Paul exhibit the gift of the working of miracles? (Acts 8:5–8, 13; 15:12; 19:11–12)

_____

_____

9. How did the Holy Spirit use the gift of prophecy to warn Paul of the persecution he would experience in Jerusalem as he testified about Jesus? (Acts 21:10–11)

_____

_____

10. The gift of discerning of spirits is that which can detect the nature, motivation, and/or presence of either human spirits, angelic beings, or demonic influences and entities. Read the passages listed below and summarize how a gift of discernment operated in the lives of God's people and showed them something they would not otherwise have known.

Discernment of the Human Spirit:

Acts 5:1–11: _____

Acts 14:8–10: _____

Discernment of Angelic Beings:

Matthew 1:20–25: _____

Acts 5:17–25: _____

Discernment of Demonic Influences and Entities:

Acts 13:6–12: _____

Acts 16:16–18: _____

11. What types of tongues (languages) might a person speak who has the gift of different kinds of tongues? (1 Corinthians 13:1)

(1) _____ (2) _____

12. Besides the special gift of different kinds of tongues, how do we know that every believer may speak in tongues in private prayer and worship to God? (1 Corinthians 14:5a)

_____

13. Why is the gift of interpretation of tongues important to the body of Christ? (1 Corinthians 14:5b)

_____

14. What special instructions did the apostle Paul give for those who have the gifts of different kinds of tongues and the interpretation of tongues? (1 Corinthians 14:13, 27–28)

_____

_____

_____

15. What do manifestations of the Holy Spirit confirm to unbelievers? (Mark 16:20; Hebrews 2:3–4)

_____

16. What additional manifestations of the Holy Spirit might God's people receive (besides a gift of prophecy)? (Acts 2:17b)

(1) _____ (2) _____

17. What was the purpose of the vision that was given to Ananias of Damascus? (Acts 9:1–19)

_____

_____

18. What was the purpose of the visions that were given to Peter and Cornelius? (Acts 10:1–11:18)

_____

_____

19. How has God used supernatural dreams and the interpretation of supernatural dreams to further His purposes?

Genesis 41: _____

_____

Matthew 2:7–15: _____

_____

20. Besides tongues, knowledge, prophesying, and teaching, what special gift may believers receive? (1 Corinthians 14:6)

_____

21. The Greek word *apokalupsis*, translated as "revelation" in English, means "disclosure" or "an uncovering" (STRONG, NASC, G602). What did Paul ask God to give the Ephesians so they could know Him better? (Ephesians 1:17b NKJV, NIV)

_____

For Further Reflection

+ What do you think is your main spiritual gift? How has God used it in your life to build up the body of Christ?

+ How has your spiritual gift enabled you and others to stand strong in the faith and to engage in spiritual warfare?

+ Perhaps you have never received the baptism with the Holy Spirit, through which you can manifest the evidence of speaking in tongues for your private prayer and worship to God, as well as be empowered by the Holy Spirit with spiritual gifts and with boldness to witness about Jesus. If you haven't, I invite you to pray this prayer:

> Heavenly Father,
>
> Jesus said that You will give us Your Holy Spirit if we ask. I ask You now to pour out Your Spirit on me, so that I may draw closer to You and receive the gifts You desire to give me for the ministry You have called me to. Thank You for answering my prayer. In Jesus' name, amen.
> (See, for example, Luke 11:9–13.)

Angels: God's Servants on Our Behalf

Introduction

This lesson will begin to cover the nature and functions of angels as they do God's work, minister to human beings, and participate in spiritual warfare. Later, in study 19, "The End of the Age and the Last Battle," we will look at the role of angels at the end of the world—in the concluding days of the old earth and the final defeat of Satan.

Once, after I had been praying for several days about many people I knew and loved who were in spiritual bondage, I had a vision in which heaven opened and chariots charged out of it. A large, powerful angel was in each of the chariots. They all came down to the earth to help people who were in bondage and to deliver them, including the families that I had been praying for. Many believers do not realize how these devoted servants of God are working on their behalf. We will now see who angels are and how they interact with God's people.

Memory Verse:

> Are [angels] *not all ministering spirits sent forth to minister for those who will inherit salvation?*
> (Hebrews 1:14)

Study Questions

1. What are the primary roles of God's angels? (Psalm 103:20b; 104:4; Hebrews 1:14)

2. Should angels receive our worship? Why or why not? (Colossians 2:8, 18; Revelation 22:8–9)

_____

_____

3. Are angels all-powerful (omnipotent)? How can we tell? (Psalm 103:20b; Daniel 10:5–13, 20–21)

_____

4. What is the angels' primary response toward God? (Psalm 103:20a; Isaiah 6:1–3; Revelation 5:8–14; 7:11–12)

_____

5. (a) What does the Bible say about the nature and position of angels in relation to Jesus? (Hebrews 1:4–14; 1 Peter 3:21b–22)

_____

_____

(b) In light of question "a," above, what does the book of Hebrews mean when it says that Jesus was made *a little lower than the angels*? (Hebrews 2:5–9; Philippians 2:5–11; Matthew 28:18)

_____

_____

6. In what way does the Bible describe the number of God's angels? (Hebrews 12:22b)

_____

7. What two realms do angels move between? (Genesis 28:12; Luke 1:11, 19, 26)

_____

8. What are two types of special angels who continually worship God at His throne?

(1) Isaiah 6:2–3: _____

(2) Ezekiel 10: _____

9. Michael is among the "*chief princes,*" or chief angels. (See Daniel 10:13.) What is the designation given to each member of this rank of angels? (1 Thessalonians 4:16b; Jude 1:9a)

_____

10. Whose name and authority did Michael invoke in fighting against the devil? Complete the following:

   Jude 1:9: "*Yet Michael the archangel, in contending with the devil…dared not bring*

   *against him a reviling accusation, but said, '*_____ _____ *rebuke you!'*"

11. Do angels work alone, or do they work with other angels? (Daniel 10:12–13, 21; Zechariah 2:3–4; Luke 1:26–38; 2:8–14; Revelation 7:2–3)

_____

12. How did God use an angel to get the attention of the prophet Balaam to prevent him from going against His will? (Numbers 22:20–35)

_____

_____

_____

13. After King David sinned by numbering his army, God sent an angel to punish Israel by putting many of the Israelites to death. When God told the angel to cease destroying, the angel stood by, waiting for his next instructions. (See 1 Chronicles 21:1–15.)

    (a) Describe the angel as it appeared to David. (1 Chronicles 21:16a)

_____

    (b) How did David and the elders react to this sight? (Verse 16b)

_____

    (c) After David had offered burnt offerings and peace offerings and had called on the Lord* (see verse 26), what did the angel do at the Lord's command? (Verse 27b)

_____

14. What did angels do for Jesus after He was tempted by the devil in the wilderness and when He earnestly prayed to God the Father in the garden of Gethsemane about His imminent crucifixion? (Matthew 4:11; Mark 1:13; Luke 22:39–43)

_____

15. List seven major responsibilities that angels carry out on behalf of God's people.

(1) Exodus 14:19–20; 23:20; Psalm 91:11–12; Daniel 6:22; Matthew 18:10:

_____

(2) Genesis 19:15–17; Acts 12:8–11:

_____

(3) Luke 1:13, 26–38; 2:10–12; Matthew 28:5–7; Acts 8:26; 10:3–8; 27:13–25; Revelation 22:16:

_____

(4) Zechariah 1–2, 4:

_____

(5) 1 Kings 19:1–8; Daniel 10:17–19:

_____

(6) Revelation 8:3–4:

_____

(7) Luke 16:22:

_____

16. (a) What was a common reaction from God's people in the New Testament when angels came to help them or deliver a message to them? (Matthew 28:1–4; Luke 1:11–12, 26–29; 2:8–9)

_____

(b) What did the angels do in answer to this reaction? (Matthew 28:5–8; Luke 1:13–14, 30; 2:10–11)

_____

17. What is one way in which we may encounter angels unknowingly? (Hebrews 13:2)

_____

18. How do angels respond when even one human being repents and accepts Jesus as Savior and Lord? (Luke 15:10)

_____

19. The Lord* told the Israelites that He would send an angel before them as they entered the Promised Land. What would this angel do for them? (Exodus 23:20b)

_____

20. What terminology does the Bible use in relation to God's angels that indicates the angels conduct warfare on God's behalf?

Genesis 32:1–2:_____

Joshua 5:14:_____

21. In many places in the Scriptures, God is referred to as the "LORD of hosts." (See, for example, Psalm 24:10.) The Hebrew word for "hosts" often refers to an army (STRONG, NASC, H6635).

(a) When the prophet Elisha and his servant were surrounded by a Syrian army of horses and chariots, the servant was afraid. Yet the prophet prayed that God would open his eyes to see what He had sent to protect them. (See 2 Kings 6:15–17a.) What had God sent? (Verse 17b)

_____

(b) How many Assyrians did the angel of the Lord kill in one night in protecting the city of Jerusalem from Israel's enemies? (2 Kings 19:35)

_____

22. What will angels be doing at the second coming of Christ? (Matthew 16:27; 24:30–31; 25:31; Mark 13:27; Luke 9:26)

_____

_____

23. What will the angels witness at the end of the age? (Luke 12:8–9)

_____

_____

For Further Reflection

- Have you ever seen an angel? If so, what role was the angel fulfilling?

- Angels fight against the devil only under the authority of the Lord*. Have you been trying to fight your difficulties, trials, and temptations in your own strength? If so, how will you approach these battles now?

- God's angels offer Him heartfelt praise and worship. Are you doing the same each day out of your love for the Lord?

Part IV

The Weapons of Our Warfare

The Whole Armor of God, Part 1

Introduction

The Bible confirms that we cannot fight the devil and his demons in our own strength. Instead, we are instructed to *"be strong in the Lord and in the power of His might"* (Ephesians 6:10). We must learn to rely fully on God and to use the spiritual gifts and heavenly armor He has provided for us to counteract the enemy's attacks. We need spiritual weapons for waging spiritual warfare. Human reasoning and physical weapons will not work. Our spiritual armor will protect us, and our training in spiritual battle will guide us, as we thwart the enemy's tactics and fight against his strongholds. In this study, we will explore the first three pieces of the armor of God, which we began to look at in study 5, as they reflect aspects of offensive and defensive spiritual weaponry. Then, in study 13, we will investigate the remaining three pieces of armor.

Memory Passage:

Therefore take up the whole armor of God, that you may be able to withstand in the evil day, and having done all, to stand. Stand therefore, having girded your waist with truth, having put on the breastplate of righteousness, and having shod your feet with the preparation of the gospel of peace; above all, taking the shield of faith with which you will be able to quench all the fiery darts of the wicked one. And take the helmet of salvation, and the sword of the Spirit, which is the word of God. (Ephesians 6:13–17)

Study Questions

1. Whose armor are we to use in spiritual warfare? (Ephesians 6:11)

   _____

2. List some military language that is used to describe God. (Psalm 18:2)

   _____

3. (a) What action did the apostle Paul urge believers to take in order to be able to stand against the wiles of the devil? (Ephesians 6:11)

   _____

   (b) What action did the apostle Paul urge believers to carry out in order to be able to "*withstand in the evil day*"? (Ephesians 6:13)

   _____

4. (a) What is the first aspect of the armor of God? (Ephesians 6:14a)

   _____

   (b) This portion of armor may also be translated as what? (Ephesians 6:14 NIV)

   _____

5. In whom is truth found? (John 1:17; 14:6)

   _____

6. How can we know the truth? (John 8:31–32 NKJV, NIV; 16:13)

   (1) _____

   (2) _____

7. What did Jesus ask the Father to do on our behalf? (John 17:17, 19)

_____

8. Where does God desire His truth to be? (Psalm 51:6a NKJV, NASB)

_____

9. List two reasons people do not obey or practice God's truth. (Romans 2:8a; 1 John 1:6, 8, 10)

(1) _____

(2) _____

10. How can we know that we belong to the truth? (1 John 3:18–19)

_____

11. What does love rejoice in? (1 Corinthians 13:6)

_____

12. What is the second piece of God's armor listed by the apostle Paul? (Ephesians 6:14b)

_____

13. (a) Whose righteousness must we have? (Romans 3:21–22; 2 Corinthians 5:21b)

_____

(b) Through whom do we receive this righteousness? (Romans 3:22; 2 Corinthians 5:21)

_____

14. (a) What cannot be a substitute for God's righteousness? (Ezekiel 33:13a; Philippians 3:9a)

_____

(b) Why is this the case? (Isaiah 64:6)

_____

15. The breastplate of a soldier's armor protected his heart, in addition to other organs. What is one crucial reason why we must guard with righteousness our spiritual "heart"—the place of our innermost motivations, desires, and resolve? (Jeremiah 17:9)

_____

16. From where do the things that defile us originate? (Matthew 15:18–20)

_____

17. How does God want our hearts to be? (Matthew 5:8a; James 4:8b)

_____

18. How can we be cleansed from our unrighteousness (defilement) when we sin? (1 John 1:9)

_____

19. What instructs us on how to live according to the righteousness of God? (2 Timothy 3:16)

_____

20. What produces the *"peaceable fruit of righteousness"* within us, if we have been trained by it? (Hebrews 12:7, 10–11 NKJV, NIV)

_____

21. (a) How should we *not* present the members of our bodies? (Romans 6:13a)

_____

(b) What two things should we present to God (1) *"as being alive from the dead,"* and (2) *"as instruments of righteousness"*? (Verse 13b)

(1) _____

(2) _____

22. What has been *"created according to God, in true righteousness and holiness,"* which we should *"put on"*? (Ephesians 4:24)

_____

23. We should consider ourselves *"_____ indeed to sin, but _____ to*

God in _____ _____ _____ _____ *"*

(Romans 6:11).

24. What does righteousness produce through Jesus Christ? (Philippians 1:11a; 2 Corinthians 9:10b)

_____

25. What does God promise to those who are righteous in Him? (Isaiah 54:17)

_____

26. (a) What is the third piece in the list of God's armor? (Ephesians 6:15b)

_____

(b) What item of clothing did Paul compare this piece to? (Ephesians 6:15a)

_____

27. What did Jesus come to give to "men," or all people on earth, according to the message the angels delivered to the shepherds the night He was born? (Luke 2:14b)

_____

28. (a) How do people enter into peace with God? (Romans 5:1)

_____

(b) At what cost was that peace achieved? (Colossians 1:20b)

_____

29. How did Jesus destroy enmity between people and bring peace and unity between them, instead? (Ephesians 2:14, 16, 18)

_____

30. (a) Jesus gave something to His disciples before He returned to heaven. What was it? (John 14:27a)

_____

(b) What did Jesus _not_ give them? (Verse 27b)

_____

31. (a) What will the peace of God accomplish for us as we offer our requests to our heavenly Father and give thanks for His help? (Philippians 4:6–7)

_____

(b) What did Paul say the Philippians should do in order for the *"God of peace"* to be with them? (Philippians 4:9)

_____

(c) Timothy had *"carefully followed"* Paul's doctrine and manner of life (see 2 Timothy 3:10a), the same teaching and example Paul had given to the Philippians. List four of Paul's spiritual attributes that we, also, should practice for the *"God of peace"* to be with us. Complete the following:

2 Timothy 3:10b: *"You have carefully followed my doctrine, manner of life, purpose,*

_____, _____, _____,

_____."

32. (a) What are we instructed to pursue? (Romans 14:19)

_____

(b) What should we endeavor to promote in our relationships with other believers? (Ephesians 4:3)

_____

33. What should we always be prepared to do, in order to share the gospel of peace with others? (1 Peter 3:15b)

_____

34. What will the *"God of peace"* accomplish for us? (Romans 16:20)

_____

For Further Reflection

+ Have you consciously applied the armor of God to your life, or have you assumed it would automatically "work" for you? Today, "take up" the armor of God—receive it from God with thanksgiving through Jesus Christ—and "put it on" in faith as you obey His Word and pursue His nature and ways.

+ Make a commitment to maintain and grow in the righteousness that God has given you through Christ by meditating on and applying the following Scriptures to your life: Romans 6:11–14; Ephesians 4:20–24; 1 John 1:8–9.

THE WHOLE ARMOR OF GOD, PART 2

Introduction

Although the *"sword of the Spirit"* (the Word of God, or the Scriptures) is listed as one piece of God's armor in Ephesians 6, it is actually the key to all of them, since it is through the Scriptures that we learn God's truth, come to understand that we need His righteousness, discover His wonderful gospel of peace, receive and build our faith, and find assurance of salvation in Christ. We must keep reading, studying, and applying the Scriptures to our lives. Then, when we have thoughts and desires that do not line up with God's Word, we will be equipped with the knowledge and wisdom to reject them immediately and to remind the devil of who we are in Christ Jesus.

Are you allowing the Bible to build your faith as you read and study it? Are you learning to rely on God's truth rather than what you see in the circumstances around you? Holding fast to the Word of God will sustain you spiritually and protect you from the enemy.

Memory Passage:

For the weapons of our warfare are not carnal but mighty in God for pulling down strongholds, casting down arguments and every high thing that exalts itself against the knowledge of God, bringing every thought into captivity to the obedience of Christ, and being ready to punish all disobedience when your obedience is fulfilled. (2 Corinthians 10:4–6)

Study Questions

35. (a) What is the fourth piece in the list of God's armor? (Ephesians 6:16a)

_____

(b) What is the main purpose of this portion of the armor? (Verse 16b)

_____

36. (a) How did the writer of the book of Hebrews define faith? (Hebrews 11:1)

_____

(b) In what manner did Paul describe how believers "walk," spiritually speaking? (2 Corinthians 5:7)

_____

37. What does our faith in Christ provide for us? (Romans 5:1–2a)

_____

38. In what way does faith come to us? (Romans 10:17)

_____

39. Satan's "fiery darts" are often aimed at our thoughts. In what two ways can we combat these attacks with the shield of faith, which is built upon the Word of God? (2 Corinthians 10:5)

(1) _____

(2) _____

40. What did Jesus reply when His disciples asked Him to increase their faith? (Luke 17:5–6)

_____

41. What is the fifth piece in the list of God's armor? (Ephesians 6:17a)

_____

42. (a) In another New Testament letter, what characteristic did Paul link with this piece of armor? (1 Thessalonians 5:8b)

_____

(b) What words does the Bible use to describe the above characteristic, giving it a different meaning from the one it usually has in contemporary society—that of something "wished for"? Complete the following:

Hebrews 6:19: "*…an* _____ *of the soul, both* _____ *and*

_____*."*

43. How do we receive the helmet of salvation? (Romans 10:9–10)

_____

_____

44. (a) We can keep our helmet of salvation securely in place by continually looking to Jesus as our righteousness and by bearing spiritual fruit through Him. As a review, what do we diligently need to build upon our faith, in order to make our *"call and election sure"* and to keep from being unfruitful in our knowledge of Jesus Christ? (2 Peter 1:5–8, 10)

_____

_____

(b) If someone lacks the above things, what does it say that he is, spiritually speaking? (2 Peter 1:9)

_____

_____

45. What assurance do we have concerning our salvation? (Hebrews 7:25)

_____

_____

46. Name the sixth piece in the list of God's armor. (Ephesians 6:17b)

_____

47. (a) The writer of Hebrews made an analogy for this piece of armor that is similar to the apostle Paul's. How did he describe the Word of God? (Hebrews 4:12a)

_____

(b) What does this weapon have the capacity to do because of its sharp discernment? (Verse 12b)

_____

48. What does the Bible say about God's Word in terms of its trustworthiness? (Psalm 19:9b; 119:160a; John 17:17b)

_____

_____

49. What must we combine with the Word of God for it to be effective in our lives—something the Israelites in the wilderness failed to "mix" with the word from God that they heard? (Hebrews 4:2b)

_____

50. Paul encouraged Timothy to preach God's Word to others—convincing, rebuking, and exhorting them with patience and careful teaching. At what times was Timothy supposed to be ready to do this? (2 Timothy 4:2)

_____

51. We need to become so familiar with the Word of God that we can use the spiritual weapon of the "sword of the Spirit" to defeat the devil's temptations, just as Jesus did, especially when the devil tries to twist the Scriptures out of context. (See Matthew 4:1–11.) With this in mind…

    (a) List two ways we should respond to God's Word. (Psalm 1:2)

(1) _____

(2) _____

    (b) When we are familiar with God's Word "*by reason of use,*" what are we able to discern? (Hebrews 5:14b)

_____

    (c) How can we present ourselves to God as approved "workers" for Him? (2 Timothy 2:15b NKJV, NIV)

_____

_____

52. (a) What kind of spiritual armor did Paul encourage the Romans to put on? (Romans 13:12b)

_____

(b) Two verses later, what did Paul tell the Romans to "put on," signifying what the above spiritual armor refers to? (Verse 14a)

_____

53. (a) What did Jesus describe Himself as? (John 8:12a)

_____

(b) Name two things that characterize those who follow Jesus. (Verse 12b)

_____

_____

For Further Reflection

+ Which of the six pieces of armor do you feel needs reinforcement in your life? Why? Using the questions from studies 12 or 13 for that portion of armor as a guideline, make a commitment to strengthen it through your faith in Christ.

+ Be prepared with God's truth so that you can stay strong as you battle against Satan and his demonic strongholds. Confess God's Word over your life in faith and receive His supernatural grace and power. You can begin with these truths:

"I am the righteousness of God in Christ." (See 2 Corinthians 5:21.)

"No weapon formed against me will prosper." (See Isaiah 54:17.)

"I can do all things through Christ who strengthens me." (See Philippians 4:13.)

Prayer, Fasting, and Praise

Introduction

Developing a close relationship with God through Christ will keep us from being caught off guard by Satan's attacks. Prayer keeps us near to God and strengthens us spiritually. The Lord* wants us to pray so that salvation, revival, deliverance, and healing can take place across the nation and around the world. Spiritual hosts of wickedness—unseen by us—rule over various spiritual territories of the earth. If they are not cast down through prayer, they will govern whatever yields to their demonic influences within those territories. And, although we may not receive an immediate answer to our prayers because of demonic resistance, we must continue to pray. As we intercede, we will receive breakthroughs. No demon or principality from hell can stop God's purposes from being fulfilled.

In addition to praying, we may need to fast when conducting spiritual warfare. Fasting, or abstaining from food for various lengths of time, should be a normal part of our Christian experience. During a fast, our spirits can hear from the Lord* in a special way. Denying the flesh* through fasting helps us to maintain the purity and power of our spiritual lives. Often, we hear more from God and learn more about Him and His ways through fasting than we ever could otherwise.

While we pray and fast, praise is a key to spiritual victory, as we exalt the One who is our King and heavenly Father and who knows our needs even before we ask Him to meet them. (See Matthew 6:8.)

Memory Verses:

Praying always with all prayer and supplication in the Spirit, being watchful to this end with all perseverance and supplication for all the saints.　　　　　(Ephesians 6:18)

"Not by might nor by power, but by My Spirit," says the LORD of hosts.   (Zechariah 4:6)

Study Questions

Prayer

1. (a) After the apostle Paul encouraged the Ephesian believers to put on the six pieces of the armor of God, what else did he say they should do? (Ephesians 6:18a)

    _____

    (b) In what manner were they to do this? (Verse 18b)

    _____

2. What additional words did the apostles Paul and Peter use to describe the manner in which believers should pray? Complete the following:

    Colossians 4:2: *"Continue* _____ *in prayer, being*

    _____ *in it...."*

    1 Peter 4:7: *"The end of all things is at hand; therefore be* _____ *and*

    watchful in your prayers."

3. What instructions did Jesus give for how we should conduct ourselves in prayer? (Matthew 6:5–7)

    _____

    _____

4. (a) With what mind-set are we to go to God in prayer? (Matthew 21:22; Mark 11:24)

    _____

(b) What should we offer to God along with our prayers and supplication? (Colossians 4:2b; Philippians 4:6)

_____

5. Name a requirement for both having a right relationship with God and receiving answers to our prayers. (Mark 11:25–26)

_____

6. (a) List six petitions that are included in the model prayer Jesus gave His disciples, also known as the Lord's Prayer.

Luke 11:2b:

(1) _____

(2) _____

Verse 3:

(3) _____

Verse 4:

(4) _____

(5) _____

(6) _____

(b) In the garden of Gethsemane, what did Jesus tell His disciples to do that corresponds to petition 5, above? (Luke 22:40)

_____

7. (a) Why is it important for us to pray for *"all men,"* especially for kings and others in positions of authority? (1 Timothy 2:1–2)

_____

   (b) What does God desire, which our prayers and the above lifestyle both promote? (Verse 4)

_____

8. Whom was God seeking among the people of the land who were sinning and oppressing others? (Ezekiel 22:29–30)

_____

_____

9. (a) What kind of prayers can we be confident that God has heard? (1 John 5:14)

_____

   (b) When we know God has heard our prayers, what else do we know? (Verse 15)

_____

10. What reason did the angel give Daniel for why the answer to his prayer was delayed? (Daniel 10:11–13)

_____

_____

11. When we need to wait for the manifestation of the answer to a prayer, we may be tempted to grow discouraged. In those cases, what should we do instead?

Luke 18:1b: _____

Romans 12:12b: _____

1 Thessalonians 5:17: _____

12. What encouraging word did the devout Cornelius receive about his prayers and generous deeds toward others? (Acts 10:4b NKJV, NIV)

_____

13. Who is continually praying for us as we minister to and pray for others?

Hebrews 7:22, 25: _____

Romans 8:26–27: _____

14. (a) In what two basic ways can we pray? (1 Corinthians 14:15a)

(1) _____

(2) _____

(b) When we pray with our spirits—in "tongues"—through whom are we praying? (Acts 2:4; 19:6)

_____

15. What phrases does the book of Acts use to describe New Testament believers receiving the Holy Spirit, through whom they were given the ability to speak in tongues? Complete the following: [continued, next page]

Acts 10:44: "…*the Holy Spirit* _____ _____ *all those who heard*

the Word."

Acts 10:45: "…*the gift of the Holy Spirit had been* _____ _____ *on*

the Gentiles."

Acts 19:6: "And when Paul had laid hands on them, the Holy Spirit _____

_____ them, and they spoke with tongues and prophesied."

16. What kind of prayer "avails much"? (James 5:16b)

_____

17. Praying alone in one's "prayer closet" or "secret place" (Matthew 6:6) is vital, yet praying together with other believers is also important. What two things did Jesus say would happen when believers joined in prayer in His name? (Matthew 18:19–20)

(1) _____

(2) _____

18. Disunity among believers prevents them from praying together effectively.

(a) Paul said he desired believers to pray everywhere, "lifting up

_____ _____" (1 Timothy 2:8).

(b) What were the believers to eliminate among themselves? (Verse 8b)

_____

19. What should we remember we are wrestling against as we engage in spiritual warfare through prayer? (Ephesians 6:12)

_____

_____

20. Taking the example of Epaphras, a first-century Christian, what should we "labor fervently" for in prayer on behalf of other people? (Colossians 4:12b)

_____

Fasting

21. What wording did Jesus use in talking about fasting that shows us He expected believers to observe this practice? Complete the following:

    Matthew 6:16: *"Moreover, _____ you fast...."*

    Luke 5:35: *"The days will come when the bridegroom [Jesus Himself] will be taken away*

    from [the disciples]; _____ _____ _____

    _____."

22. (a) In what way do some people fast hypocritically? (Matthew 6:16)

    _____

    (b) To whom alone should we fast? Complete the following:

    Matthew 6:18a: *"Your* _____ *who is in the*

    _____ _____."

    (c) How will the Father respond when we fast in the right manner? (Verse 18b)

    _____

23. What did Jesus do before being tempted by the devil? (Matthew 4:1–2)

    _____

24. After casting out a certain kind of demon from an epileptic boy, what did Jesus tell His disciples that made a connection between fasting with spiritual warfare? (Matthew 17:14–21)

    _____

The Bible records many occasions when God's people fasted. We will look briefly at three of those occasions in questions 25–27 of this study.

25. (a) Whom did Queen Esther ask to fast for three days on her behalf before she approached the king to plead for the lives of her people? (Esther 4:15–16)

_____

(b) In two or three sentences, summarize the ultimate outcome of this fast. (Esther 8–9)

_____

_____

_____

26. (a) What position did Nehemiah hold in service to King Artaxerxes of Persia? (Nehemiah 1:11b)

_____

(b) What did Nehemiah do when he heard that the remnant of Jews in Jerusalem who had not been carried into captivity were in *great distress and reproach,* and that the wall of the city was broken down and that its gates had been burned? (Nehemiah 1:4b)

_____

(c) Complete the following excerpts from Nehemiah's prayer to God that reflect important elements of prayer: [continued, next page]

(1) *Praise and Worship*:

Nehemiah 1:5: "Lord God of heaven, O _____ and _____

God...."

(2) *Confession:*

Nehemiah 1:6: *"I...confess the _____ of the children of Israel which we have*

sinned against _____."

(3) *God's Word:*

Nehemiah 1:8: *"Remember, I pray, the _____ that _____*

_____ Your servant Moses...."

27. After Nehemiah had fasted and prayed, what response did he receive from the king when he requested a leave of absence and safe passage to Judah to rebuild the wall of Jerusalem, as well as materials for the rebuilding? (Nehemiah 2:4–8)

_____

_____

28. (a) What was the Roman centurion Cornelius doing before the angel appeared to him, which led to his salvation through Peter's ministry? (Acts 10:30)

_____

(b) As a review from the earlier "Prayer" portion of this study, what did the angel tell Cornelius were remembered in the sight of God? (Verse 31 NKJV, NIV)

_____

29. (a) True fasting is not just depriving ourselves of food (see Isaiah 58:5) but aligning ourselves with God's priorities, desires, and will. What kind of fast did God say He desires from us? (Isaiah 58:6–7)

_____

_____

(b) What is the result of such a fast? (Isaiah 58:8–9b)

_____

Praise

30. In Psalm 18, David wrote about calling upon the Lord* when he was being pursued by his enemies.

    (a) What did David say the Lord* is worthy of? (Verse 3a)

    _____

    (b) What did David say would be the result of his calling upon the Lord* in praise? (Verse 3b)

    _____

31. In Psalm 40, what did David say would be the result when people heard him praising the Lord* for delivering and establishing him? (Psalm 40:3b)

    _____

32. What two forms of audible praise were involved in the Israelites' victory over the city of Jericho? (Joshua 6:4–5)

(1) _____

(2) _____

33. (a) After encouraging the people of Judah to believe in the Lord* their God, what did King Jehoshaphat appoint certain people to do when the nation was faced with fighting their enemies? (2 Chronicles 20:21a)

    _____

    (b) What words did they use? (Verse 21b)

    _____

(c) What resulted when they began to sing and praise? (Verse 22)

34. In Acts 16, there is an account of Paul and Silas being miraculously freed from their imprisonment and then leading the jailer and his family to salvation. (See Acts 16:26–33.) What were Paul and Silas doing just before these events? (Verse 25)

35. There is a spiritual "garment" that can we "put on" for waging spiritual warfare against "*the spirit of heaviness*," or depression and despair. What is it called? (Isaiah 61:3)

36. What did the writer of Hebrews say we should continually offer to God through Jesus Christ? (Hebrews 13:15)

For Further Reflection

+ Shortly before His crucifixion, Jesus prayed to the Father for believers, that (1) we would be kept spiritually through the powerful name of God, (2) we would have the same joy He has, (3) we would be kept from the evil one, (4) we would be sanctified by God's truth, (5) we would have unity with other believers and with the Father and the Son*, (6) we would be witnesses to the world of the truth of the gospel because of this unity, and (7) one day we would live with Jesus and see His glory. (See John 17:9–24.) As you pray, you can intercede along the same lines for yourself and others.

+ If you have not yet done so, ask God to baptize you with His Holy Spirit, so that you can pray to Him through a Spirit-given prayer language in the "*tongues of men and of angels*" (1 Corinthians 13:1) as you address in prayer the needs in your life and in the lives of others.

+ After Jesus fasted for forty days in the wilderness, He was tempted by the devil. (See Matthew 4:1–11.) When you fast, be especially alert to any attacks and temptations from Satan, through which he will attempt to hinder your prayers and harm your relationship with God.

+ Incorporate praise and thanksgiving into your prayer life through psalms such as these: Psalms 18, 33, and 136.

The Name of Jesus

Introduction

We must follow the archangel Michael's example when waging spiritual warfare by rebuking Satan in the name of the Lord*. (See Jude 1:9.) In this way, we can break the strongholds the enemy uses to bind us in fear, anger, discouragement, sickness, and oppression. Demons tremble at Jesus' name and flee from His presence.

Once, in a vision, I saw demonic powers hovering over a certain state. They were huge creatures—they looked about fifty feet high—and they were resting upon seven large cement thrones. They were all in a circle, mumbling to each other.

God said to me, "This is the prince of the power of the air, the rulers of demon darkness, the spiritual wickedness in high places that sit in the heavens above the earth. They cause chaos in the lives of people and brainwash those who acquiesce to their ungodly influences. I want you to see this, understand it, and tell the world about it. Explain to them that, in the name of Jesus, they have the authority and the power to pull this evil kingdom down."

As I prepared to pray, the Lord* reminded me, "Whatever you bind on earth is bound in heaven, and whatever you loose on earth is loosed in heaven. [See Matthew 16:19; 18:18.] Take dominion over these things and bind them. Command them to fall off their thrones, in the name of Jesus and by the blood of Jesus Christ."

When we do this, angels descend from heaven. I have seen them circle these demons, put chains around them, and yank them from their thrones. One by one, the demons have fallen as the angels of God dragged them away. The angels were shouting and praising the Lord* in the name of Jesus Christ.

Regardless of what demonic weapons are used against us, when we know how to rebuke the devil in the name of Jesus, these weapons will not be successful. Believers all over the world can call upon Jesus' name as it is spelled or pronounced in their native languages, such as Yeshua (Hebrew), Jesús (Spanish), Gesù (Italian), Íosa (Irish), Xesús (Galician), Yesu (Swahili), or Chúa Giêsu (Vietnamese). The authority and power reside in Jesus Himself, our King and Redeemer.

Memory Passage:

Therefore God also has highly exalted Him and given Him the name which is above every name, that at the name of Jesus every knee should bow, of those in heaven, and of those on earth, and of those under the earth, and that every tongue should confess that Jesus Christ is Lord, to the glory of God the Father. (Philippians 2:9–11)

Study Questions

1. What did the meaning of Jesus' name signify about His purpose on earth? (Matthew 1:21b)

   _____

2. In the Scriptures, Jesus is depicted by various titles and designations, all of which reflect aspects of His nature and the salvation He came to bring. List some of these titles and designations.

Isaiah 9:6b: _____

   _____

Malachi 4:2a: _____

John 1:29b: _____

John 6:35a: _____

John 10:11: _____

John 14:6a: _____

Revelation 22:13, 16b: _____

_____

3. In whose name (authority) did Jesus operate in His ministry on earth? (John 10:25b; 12:49; 14:10)

_____

4. What two things was Jesus subsequently given by the Father? (Matthew 28:18; Philippians 2:9)

_____

_____

5. (a) What is possible only in the name of Jesus? (Acts 4:12)

_____

(b) Name two eternal spiritual gifts we receive in Jesus' name.

(1) John 14:26a: _____

(2) John 20:31b: _____

6. Jesus has given to His followers power and authority over various aspects of evil and danger, such as these indicated in the gospel of Luke.

Luke 9:1: _____

Luke 10:19: _____

7. In light of our authority in Jesus' name, what effect do our actions on earth produce in heaven? (Matthew 18:18)

_____

_____

8. (a) How did Jesus say He would respond to what we ask in His name (authority)? Complete the following:

John 14:13: *"And whatever you ask in My name,* _____ _____ _____ _____*."*

John 14:14: *"If you ask anything in My name,* _____ _____ _____ _____*."*

(b) For what ultimate purpose does Jesus grant what we ask in His name? (Verse 13b)

_____

9. What is a prerequisite for receiving whatever we request in Jesus' name? (John 15:16a)

_____

10. What "signs" will follow those who believe in Jesus as they minister in His name? (Mark 16:17–18)

_____

_____

11. Describe a few of the miraculous works that believers manifested in the New Testament. [continued, next page]

Acts 16:16–18; 19:11–12: _____

_____

Acts 2:1–4; 10:44–46a: _____

_____

Acts 28:3–6: _____

Acts 3:1–8; Acts 28:8: _____

_____

12. What was required, along with the authority of Jesus' name, for the lame man to be healed? (Acts 3:16)

_____

13. (a) What did the religious leaders recognize about Peter and John that convinced them these two men were not qualified in their own power to heal a lame man? Complete the following:

Acts 4:13a: "*…they perceived that* [Peter and John] *were* _____ *and*

_____ *men.*"

(b) What did they suddenly understand was the reason Peter and John had succeeded in healing him? Complete the following:

Acts 4:13b: "*And they realized that* _____ _____ _____

_____ _____."

14. John rebuked someone who was outside of the circle of Jesus' immediate disciples for casting out demons in Jesus' name. (See Mark 9:38.) In essence, what was Jesus' response when John told Him about it? (Mark 9:39–40)

_____

_____

15. (a) Some people use the name of Jesus as if it were a "magic formula" for getting what they want. In the biblical account of the sons of Sceva, we see what can happen to those who take Jesus' name too lightly. (See Acts 19:13–17.) What did the evil spirit reply to the sons of Sceva, indicating that in order to use the name of Jesus with authority, we have to have a true relationship with Jesus that is evident even to demons? (Acts 19:15)

_____

(b) What was the Ephesians' response after they realized the great power of Jesus' name when it is used with genuine authority? (Verse 17b)

_____

16. (a) Describe some of the opposition Jesus' followers experienced from the authorities after doing miracles and preaching in Jesus' name. (Acts 4:18, 21a; 5:40b; 9:29; 26:10)

_____

(b) Indicate below how Peter and John responded to the officials and to God when they were commanded not to speak or teach in the name of Jesus. [continued, next page]

(1) To the officials: (Acts 4:20)

_____

(2) To God: (Acts 4:29–30)

_____

_____

(c) After they were imprisoned for the gospel and then miraculously delivered, what did Peter and the other apostles say to the officials who questioned them? (Acts 5:29)

_____

17. What does Jesus promise to those who experience loss for the sake of His name? (Matthew 19:29)

_____

_____

18. Read Psalm 20:6–8. What are we to put our trust in, rather than the power of this world? (Verse 7b)

_____

19. (a) How is the name of the Lord* depicted in Proverbs? (Proverbs 18:10a)

_____

(b) What is the condition of the righteous who run to it? (Proverbs 18:10b)

_____

20. How are we to respond, regardless of any opposition or persecution we experience, as Jesus commended the church in Pergamos for doing? Complete the following:

Revelation 2:13b: *"And you* _____ _____ _____ _____

_____, *and* _____ _____ _____ _____

_____ *even in the days in which Antipas was My faithful martyr, who was*

killed among you, where Satan dwells."

21. What exhortation did Paul give to the Colossians, indicating that our entire lives are to be lived under Jesus' authority and on His behalf? (Colossians 3:17a)

_____

For Further Reflection

- Reread the following Scriptures related to the titles and designations given to Jesus, in order to build your faith in what He desires to do for you and on behalf of others: Isaiah 9:6; Malachi 4:2; John 1:29; 6:35; 10:11; 14:6; Revelation 22:13, 16.

- In this lesson, we have seen that three qualifications for using the authority of Jesus' name are having faith in His name, bearing spiritual fruit consistently, and having a genuine, established relationship with Jesus. Otherwise, we end up treating His name like a "magic formula" to get what we want. Being honest with yourself, have you fulfilled the above conditions for doing the work of God in Jesus' name? Or, have you been treating the name of Jesus as a formula? If you answered yes to the latter, begin today to strengthen your relationship with Jesus and to build trust in His Word while aligning your priorities with His, in preparation to do the works He calls His followers to do.

The Blood of the Lamb

Introduction

In the sport of bowling, the object is to knock down the pins that are lined up at the end of the lane. As you throw the ball toward the pins, the ball may sometimes roll into the gutter. But your goal is to hit the front pin, so that it will fall and knock over all the other pins, as well. This is the way I look at spiritual warfare. If we deal with evil spirits directly, by striking them with the power of Jesus Christ, they will respond by falling over in defeat. They cannot stand against the name of Jesus and the blood He shed on our behalf.

Jesus Christ has infinitely greater power than the *"prince of the power of the air"* (Ephesians 2:2) and his evil demons. The Lord* watches over us as we apply the blood of Jesus, the Lamb of God, to all aspects of our lives and in every difficult situation we face. Through the name of Jesus, and by His shed blood, we can have authority over all the power of the enemy.

Memory Passages:

In Him we have redemption through His blood, the forgiveness of sins, according to the riches of His grace. (Ephesians 1:7)

Then I heard a loud voice saying in heaven, "Now salvation, and strength, and the kingdom of our God, and the power of His Christ have come, for the accuser of our brethren, who accused them before our God day and night, has been cast down. And they overcame him by the blood of the Lamb and by the word of their testimony, and they did not love their lives to the death." (Revelation 12:10–11)

Study Questions

1. The blood that Jesus shed on the cross is the *"blood of the* _____

   _____*"* (Matthew 26:28).

2. The old covenant was essentially based on the Israelites' ability to keep God's law—all of His commandments. (See Exodus 24:3–8.) How well did the Israelites do this? Explain. (Psalm 78:10, 37a)

   _____

   _____

3. An important practice under the old covenant—a forerunner to Jesus' sacrifice on the cross—was the sacrifice of animals on the altar of the tabernacle and, later, the temple. This occurred twice daily, as well as during special holy days, such as the Day of Atonement. What was the purpose of the animal sacrifices? (Leviticus 16:30b)

   _____

4. The Bible tells us that the old covenant under the law was "faulty" in keeping the Israelites in right relationship with God, so that a new covenant was needed. (See Hebrews 8:7.) Complete the following list of reasons why the old covenant was not sufficient:

   (a) Hebrews 8:9: *"…because* [the Israelites] _____ _____

   _____ _____ *My covenant, and I disregarded them,*

   says the Lord.*"*

(b) Hebrews 10:4: *"It is _____ _____ that the blood of bulls*

and goats could _____ _____ _____."

(c) Hebrews 10:1: *"For the law...can _____ with these same sacrifices,*

which they offer continually year by year, _____ those who approach

_____."

5. How was Christ's sacrifice on the cross fully and eternally sufficient, removing our sins permanently and enabling us to be restored to unbroken relationship with God? Complete the following:

(a) Hebrews 10:10: *"We have been sanctified through the offering of the body of Jesus*

Christ _____ _____ _____."

(b) Hebrews 10:12–14: *"But this Man, after He had offered _____*

_____ for sins forever, sat down at the right hand of God, from

that time waiting till His enemies are made His footstool. For by one offering He has

_____ _____ those who are being sanctified."

6. What did God say to explain the nature of the new covenant through Jesus' blood, by which we are perfected in Him? (Hebrews 10:16–17)

_____

_____

7. What was each Hebrew family to sacrifice on the first Passover night, when the Israelites were delivered from Egyptian slavery? (Exodus 12:3, 5–6)

_____

8. What did the Lord* say would be the effect of the blood of the lambs, which was to be applied to the doorposts and lintels (see Exodus 12:7) of the Israelites' homes that first Passover? (Exodus 12:12–13)

_____

_____

9. What statement did the apostle Paul make in which he compared Jesus to the Passover lamb? (1 Corinthians 5:7b)

_____

10. Recall that only one type of sacrifice was acceptable before God for the forgiveness of sins. Complete the following:

    Exodus 12:5a: *"Your lamb shall be _____ _____."*

11. In what way did the apostle Peter describe Jesus that used the same analogy of a lamb that Paul used? (1 Peter 1:19b)

_____

12. For what reason could Jesus be described in the above way? (Hebrews 4:15b)

_____

13. To better understand why it was necessary for forgiveness and salvation to come through the shedding of blood, complete the following:

  (a) Leviticus 17:11a: *"For the* _____ *of the flesh is* _____

  _____ _____."

  (b) Leviticus 17:11b: *"It is the blood that* _____

  _____ *for the soul."*

  (c) Hebrews 9:22b: *"Without shedding of blood there is* _____

  _____."

14. What does Jesus' blood do for us that can be compared to what the blood of the Passover lambs did for the Israelites in Egypt? (Romans 5:9)

  _____

15. Through what do we "apply" Jesus' blood to our lives in order to receive salvation? Complete the following:

  Romans 3:24b–25: *"Christ Jesus, whom God set forth as a propitiation by His blood,*

  _____ _____."

16. Unlike the old covenant, which was temporary, what kind of covenant did Jesus provide through His blood? (Hebrews 13:20b)

  _____

17.   What has Jesus accomplished in heaven and on earth through His shed blood?

Colossians 1:19–20: _____

Revelation 5:9b: _____

_____

18.   In the Old Testament, only the high priest was allowed to go into the Most Holy Place (the Holiest), where the presence of God dwelled between the cherubim above the ark of the covenant—and that only once a year. Since Jesus shed His blood, what can every believer have the boldness to do? (Hebrews 10:19)

_____

19.   (a) What does the blood of Christ cleanse our consciences from? (Hebrews 9:14b)

_____

(b) Having been cleansed, what are we able to do? (Hebrews 9:14b)

_____

20.   What four benefits have come to us due to the defeat of *the accuser of* [the] *brethren* (Satan) by the blood of Jesus? (Revelation 12:10a)

(1) _____ (2) _____

(3) _____

(4) _____

21.   What does the blood of Jesus do for us as we walk according to God's light? (1 John 1:7b)

_____

22. After we have been cleansed in the blood of Jesus, what must we remember when the accuser tries to charge us with failing to live up to the requirements of God's law? (Romans 8:1–2)

_____

23. (a) What image is used in the book of Zechariah that can remind us of what Jesus has done for us through the new covenant in His blood, especially in delivering us from the bondage of Satan? (Zechariah 9:11b)

_____

(b) What are the *"prisoners of hope"* told to do? (Verse 12a NKJV, NIV)

_____

(c) What did God promise these former prisoners? (Verse 12b)

_____

24. As the sacrificial Lamb who shed His blood for our sins, Jesus is worthy to receive what? (Revelation 5:12b)

_____

_____

For Further Reflection

+ How often do you express appreciation to Jesus for all that He did for you on the cross? Offer sincere thanks to Him for shedding His blood on your behalf, providing you with forgiveness of sins, freeing you from the bondage of Satan, and allowing you free access to your heavenly Father.

+ Have you ever had someone tell you to "plead the blood of Jesus" over a specific problem in your life? Perhaps you're wondering what this phrase means. It means to ask God, in faith and reverence, to apply all that Jesus' shed blood accomplished to your own life and the lives of your loved ones. Jesus' blood is powerful, as we have seen in this study. You can begin by praying a prayer such as this: "Lord, I believe I have the victory through Christ in every area of my life. I repent of my sins. [Name them.] I ask You to cover me and my entire household with Jesus' blood and Your Word, so that no weapons formed against us will prosper. Hold me close to You; teach me and guide me today. In the name of Jesus, and through His precious blood, amen."

+ The power of the blood of Jesus is the key to defeating Satan. In addition to your prayers, you can make statements of faith based on God's Word that confirm your reliance on the blood of the Lamb, such as "Jesus' blood covers my household" (see Exodus 12:13; Acts 16:31), or "Jesus' blood cleanses my conscience from dead works, so that I can serve the living God" (see Hebrews 9:14).

The Word of Our Testimony

Introduction

The more you pay attention to God's truth in the Scriptures and apply it to your life, the more the enemy must flee and make way for the blessings of God to come upon you. Revelation 12:10 says that believers in Jesus overcame the devil by both the blood of the Lamb and the word of their testimony. The term *"testimony"* in this verse can mean "evidence given," "record," "report," or "witness" (STRONG, G3141).

In Revelation 19:13, we read that "[Jesus] *was clothed with a robe dipped in blood, and His name is called The Word of God.*" The blood and the Word are active on our behalf as we first receive them and then testify to the truth of the gospel of Jesus Christ with our words and our actions. The devil cannot stand up to the truth of God in Jesus Christ!

Memory Passages:

Always be ready to give a defense to everyone who asks you a reason for the hope that is in you, with meekness and fear; having a good conscience….   (1 Peter 3:15–16a)

I am not ashamed of the gospel of Christ, for it is the power of God to salvation for everyone who believes, for the Jew first and also for the Greek.   (Romans 1:16)

Study Questions

1. What kind of a witness is Jesus described as? (Revelation 1:5a; 3:14)

2. What did John the Baptist say that Jesus testified about? (John 3:32)

_____

3. What did Jesus say He had been born and had come into the world to bear witness to? (John 18:37)

_____

4. Who hears Jesus' voice? (John 18:37b)

_____

5. What did Jesus' own works bear witness of? (John 5:36)

_____

6. What do true followers of Jesus "keep" and "have"? (Revelation 12:17b)

(a) They keep... _____

(b) They have... _____

7. What testimony has God made concerning us and Jesus? (1 John 5:11)

_____

8. The message of the gospel of salvation was first spoken by Jesus. Who confirmed Jesus' words to the writer of Hebrews and to others who came to believe, even though most of them had not personally seen Jesus? (Hebrews 2:3b)

_____

9. What qualifications did those who were with Jesus from the beginning have as credible witnesses of Him? Complete the following:

   1 John 1:1: *"That which was from the beginning, which we have _____, which*

   we have _____ with our eyes, which we have _____

   _____, and our hands have _____, concerning the Word

   of life...."

10. Who is always available to testify about Jesus to us? (John 15:26)

   _____

11. Name something the Holy Spirit bears witness to in regard to our identity in Christ. (Romans 8:16b)

   _____

12. (a) How did Paul describe Apollos, Peter, and himself? (1 Corinthians 4:1)

   _____

   (b) What is required of stewards? (Verse 2)

   _____

13. In what ways did God confirm the authenticity of the gospel as proclaimed by the followers of Jesus, the same as He did for Jesus Himself? (Acts 14:3b; Romans 15:19a; Hebrews 2:3–4)

   _____

14. (a) By what did the patriarchs and other believers in the past obtain a good testimony? (Hebrews 11:1–2)

_____

(b) By what did Abel obtain a righteous testimony? (Verse 4a)

_____

(c) By what did Enoch obtain the testimony that he *"pleased God"*? (Verse 5)

_____

15. For what did Paul commend the Romans and the Thessalonians, respectively? Complete the following:

(a) Romans 1:8: *"I thank my God through Jesus Christ for you all, that your*

_____ *is spoken of throughout the whole world."*

(b) 1 Thessalonians 1:8: *"For from you the* _____ _____ _____

_____ *has sounded forth…in every place. Your* _____ *toward*

God has gone out."

16. (a) What did David say He had *not* hidden and concealed? (Psalm 40:10)

_____

_____

(b) What had he declared? (Verse 10)

_____

17. (a) Recall what the apostle Peter said we should always be ready to give. (1 Peter 3:15)

_____

(b) With what attitudes and condition are we to give it? (Verses 15b–16 NKJV, NIV)

_____

18. Jesus warned His disciples that they would be persecuted, beaten, seized, and taken before religious and political leaders for a reason—as a testimony to them. Under these circumstances…

(a) What did Jesus tell them not to worry about or try to plan ahead for when this happened? (Matthew 10:19a; Mark 13:11a; Luke 21:14)

_____

(b) Instead, what did He tell them they should do? (Matthew 10:19b–20; Mark 13:11b; Luke 21:15)

_____

19. Why was Paul not ashamed of the gospel of Christ? (Romans 1:16)

_____

20. Paul exhorted believers to be wise in their interactions with those who are outside of the faith. What did he say our speech should always be, so that we may know how we should answer each person? (Colossians 4:5–6)

_____

21. While all believers should have a good testimony, who in the church are especially responsible for having a good testimony in the communities in which they live? (1 Timothy 3:2, 7–9 NKJV, NIV)

_____

22. (a) How should we respond to those who oppose the teaching and testimony of the true gospel, and for what purpose should we respond in this way? (2 Timothy 2:24b–26a)

_____

_____

(b) What has the devil taken them captive to do? (Verse 26b)

_____

(c) How are we to respond to a divisive person who persists in his divisiveness, even after being warned about it? (Titus 3:10) What is the condition of such a person? (Verse 11)

_____

23. (a) How did Paul describe those who are living a false witness in relation to the gospel? (2 Timothy 3:5a)

_____

(b) What do they resist? (Verse 8a)

_____

(c) How are their minds described? (Verse 8b)

_____

24. What should we take into consideration as we endeavor to evaluate whether a spiritual leader has genuine faith? Complete the following:

Hebrews 13:7b: "_Whose faith follow, considering the_ _____ _of_

their _____."

25. (a) What should those who have believed in God be careful to maintain? (Titus 3:8b)

_____

(b) What is our faith (or testimony), if it lacks accompanying works? (James 2:20, 26)

_____

26. List some examples of good works that believers carry out. (Matthew 25:34–36; James 1:27a)

_____

_____

_____

27. What proclamation and warning did Jesus give us? (Matthew 10:32–33)

_____

_____

28. (a) What is the ultimate sacrifice some believers have paid, and why have they paid it? (Revelation 6:9)

_____

(b) What was said about the believers who overcame Satan by the blood of the lamb and the word of their testimony? (Revelation 12:11b)

_____

29. (a) (1) Whom did Jesus say we *should not* fear? (Matthew 10:28)

_____

(2) Whom did He say we *should* fear? (Matthew 10:28)

_____

(b) What did Jesus say to encourage us that God is with us and is aware of what we are going through, even when we're persecuted for being His witnesses? (Matthew 10:29–31)

_____

_____

30. What spirit should we ask God to manifest in us when we testify about Jesus? (2 Timothy 1:7b)

_____

31. What does Christ remain toward us, even when we are faithless? Why? (2 Timothy 2:13)

_____

32. How can we regain a good testimony before God after we have been faithless or have sinned in another way? (1 John 1:7, 9)

_____

_____

33. (a) What did Paul say was confirmed in the Corinthians? (1 Corinthians 1:6)

_____

(b) Whom did he say would continue to confirm them *"to the end"*? (Verses 7–8)

_____

34. How can we become true witnesses to a transformed life in Jesus Christ, so that we *"shine as lights in the world"* as we *"hold fast the word of life"*? (Philippians 2:14–16a)

_____

_____

_____

For Further Reflection

+ Are you *"ready to give a defense to everyone who asks you a reason for the hope that is in you"* (1 Peter 3:15)? Take some time to think through your testimony of how you came to faith in Christ and what He has done in your life. Then, think about how you would communicate your testimony to someone else. You may want to write it down and review it, as you prepare to share it with those around you.

+ After you have done the above, ask the Lord to bring people into your life with whom you can share the gospel and your testimony of how Jesus has redeemed you.

+ Do you often speak about Jesus but neglect to do good works for others in His name? If so, reread Matthew 25:34–36, James 1:27; 2:20, 26, and Titus 3:8. Ask God to forgive you and to help you demonstrate the evidence of your faith as you show compassion to others in practical ways. Accept His forgiveness and seek opportunities for serving others in His name.

PART V

FINAL VICTORY

A Good Soldier of Jesus Christ

Introduction

To be "good soldiers" of Jesus Christ, we must pay close attention to God's purpose of bringing His kingdom to earth as it is in heaven. As we will see in this study, remaining alert and focused is a big part of a soldier's job. Satan is continually trying to distract us and pull us away from God's thoughts and ways. He did the same to Jesus. At one time, Peter told Jesus that He should not talk about suffering and dying on the cross. Jesus replied—knowing who was really behind Peter's statement—"*Get behind Me, Satan! For you are not mindful of the things of God, but the things of men*" (Mark 8:33).

We must be mindful of the things of God. We do this by continually submitting to His will and not allowing our lives to be steered by fear of the attacks and accusations of the devil or to be influenced by worldly concerns. It is our heritage as believers in Christ Jesus to walk in liberty and power, as well as to have victory over the devil's devices and every foe he sends on assignment against us.

The gates of hell will not prevail against the principles of God's Word. Seek God's ways and learn His Word in order to discover these principles and put them into practice. If we remain grounded on the foundation He has set forth for us to follow, the enemy will not gain the victory over us. Always remember these truths: God is with you. God loves you. God will sustain you.

Memory Passage:

You therefore must endure hardship as a good soldier of Jesus Christ. No one engaged in warfare entangles himself with the affairs of this life, that he may please him who enlisted him as a soldier.
(2 Timothy 2:3–4)

Study Questions

1. Believers fulfill various roles in relation to God and other believers. Which three roles did Paul mention when referring to his friend Epaphroditus? (Philippians 2:25a)

(1) _____ ; (2) _____ ; (3) _____

2. (a) In connection with the third role, above, what did Paul tell Timothy to do? (1 Timothy 6:12a)

_____

(b) What will this result in? Complete the following:

1 Timothy 6:12a: "Lay[ing] hold on _____."

3. What is one way a soldier can please his commanding officer? (2 Timothy 2:4 NKJV, NIV)

_____

4. What attitudes did Jesus maintain in conjunction with His mission? Complete the following:

Philippians 2:7–8: "[He]…made Himself of _____ _____,

taking the form of a _____, and coming in the likeness

of men. And being found in appearance as a man, He _____

_____ and _____ to the

point of death."

5. In the parable of the sower, Jesus compared the *"cares of this world"* and *"the deceitfulness of riches"*—things that distract people from the will of God—to thorns. What do these "thorns" do to a person? (Matthew 13:22b)

   _____

6. Why will some people depart from the faith in the end times? (1 Timothy 4:1b)

   _____

7. What three major commands did Jesus give us, which will help us to avoid being distracted from our faith and even departing from it?

(1) Matthew 6:33: _____

   _____

(2) Mark 12:30:_____

   _____

(3) Mark 12:31: _____

8. (a) In what way can we consistently bear fruit for God in our lives? (John 15:4–5)

   _____

   (b) What can we do without Jesus? (Verse 5b)

   _____

   (c) To what did Jesus compare a person who does not abide in Him? (Verse 6)

   _____

9. (a) What three things did Jesus tell us to do in anticipation of His return, since we do not know when that will be? (Mark 13:33)

(1) _____ _____ ; (2) _____

(3) _____

(b) What terms did Paul use to describe the manner in which we should live as we look for Jesus' return? (Titus 2:12b NKJV, NIV)

(1) _____

(2) _____

(3) _____

10. (a) Since *"the days are evil"* (Ephesians 5:15), how should we walk, spiritually speaking? Complete the following:

Ephesians 5:15–16: *"See then that you walk _____,*

not as fools but as wise, _____ _____

_____*...."*

(b) How can we avoid being unwise? (Verse 17)

_____

11. What is a *"good soldier of Jesus Christ"* required to do? (2 Timothy 2:3)

_____

12. To meet the above requirement, what do we first need to do, like the builder in Jesus' parable from Luke 14:28–30? (Verse 28b)

_____

13. As we have discussed in previous studies, what is often included in the cost of following Christ? (2 Timothy 3:12)

_____

14. Enduring hardship because of our faith takes fortitude and constancy.

    (a) What did Paul urge the Philippian believers to do in this regard? (Philippians 2:12b)

_____

    (b) What did Paul indicate the Philippians always did, which would be a key to their fulfilling the above exhortation? Complete the following:

    Philippians 2:12a: *"Therefore, my beloved, as you have always _____...."*

    (c) As we fulfill the answers to numbers (a) and (b), above, what must we remember? (Verse 13)

_____

15. (a) What did Paul say our *"light affliction"* is *"working"* for us? (2 Corinthians 4:17)

_____

    (b) What are we to avoid "looking at" while enduring affliction? Why? (Verse 18)

_____

    (c) What are we to look at? Why? (Verse 18)

_____

16. In Matthew 13:20–21, Jesus signified that we need to be "rooted" if we are to stay true when tribulation or persecution arises because of our faith. What instruction did Paul give for how we can do this? Complete the following:

(a) Colossians 2:6: *"As you therefore _____ _____ Christ Jesus the Lord, _____ _____ _____ _____."*

(b) Colossians 2:7: *"Rooted and _____ _____ in Him and _____ in the faith as you have been taught, abounding in it with _____."*

17. (a) What did the Lord* tell the apostle Paul in order to encourage him when he felt spiritually weak? (2 Corinthians 12:9a)

_____

_____

(b) Why did Paul say that he would *"boast"* in his infirmities? (Verse 9b)

_____

(c) What did Paul affirm, based on the above? (Verse 10b)

_____

18. Our fellow soldiers of Jesus Christ may struggle, in various ways, to *"fight the good fight of faith"* (1 Timothy 6:12).

    (a) How should we respond to a fellow believer if he is overtaken by any sin? (Galatians 6:1)

    _____

    _____

    (b) How do we fulfill the law of Christ? (Verse 2)

    _____

19. How should someone who is spiritually strong treat another believer who is spiritually weaker in matters of conscience? (Romans 15:1–2 NKJV, NIV)

    _____

    _____

20. What is the result when someone restores a believer after he has wandered away from the truth? (James 5:19–20)

    _____

21. What can those who love God and are the called according to His purpose be confident of? (Romans 8:28)

    _____

22. (a) What has God promised us, no matter what we go through? (Hebrews 13:5b)

    _____

(b) What confident affirmation can we make in response to this promise, as the writer of Hebrews did when he quoted Psalm 118? (Hebrews 13:6)

_____

_____

23. (a) When we have been *born of God,* what do we overcome? (1 John 5:4a)

_____

(b) What is the victory by which we have overcome it? (Verse 4b)

_____

24. What are we instructed to do, based on the knowledge that we already have the victory in our Lord Jesus Christ? (1 Corinthians 15:57–58)

_____

_____

25. If we offer thanksgiving to God and fulfill our responsibilities toward Him, what will He do for us when we call upon Him in the day of trouble? (Psalm 50:14–15)

_____

26. (a) Based on Paul's prayer for the Thessalonians, what can we pray for God to do for us in order to make us "good soldiers of Jesus Christ"? (2 Thessalonians 1:11)

_____

_____

(b) What will be the result of this prayer being fulfilled in our lives? (Verse 12)

_____

_____

For Further Reflection

+ Have you become "entangled" in the things of this world, so that you cannot focus on your calling as a soldier of Jesus Christ? What distractions are hindering you from seeking God's kingdom first in your life? How will you refocus your thinking and alter your lifestyle?

+ Do you know a "fellow soldier" who is currently struggling to fight the good fight of faith? Commit to pray for that person diligently, bearing his burden in prayer and seeking to restore him in a spirit of gentleness if he has been overtaken by any sin.

+ Ask the Lord to be strong in your life where you are weak, knowing that His grace is sufficient for you and that His strength is made perfect in weakness.

+ Pray Psalm 91 and other Scriptures for protection and preservation in spiritual warfare.

The End of the Age and the Last Battle

Introduction

Spiritual warfare against Satan is an ongoing reality in our lives. Yet there will come a time when the last battle of this war will be fought and the devil will be completely defeated. Satan will refuse to give up his rule over this world without a strategic fight. Yet, as the apostle Paul wrote, *"the God of peace will crush Satan under your feet shortly"* (Romans 16:20).

Jesus told us there is an *"everlasting fire prepared for the devil and his angels"* (Matthew 25:41). Hell was intended for Satan and the angels who followed him in his rebellion against God. It was not originally prepared for human beings. However, since Satan has enticed people to rebel against God and follow him, those who do not love and serve God—who continue to follow their own ways, reject God's commandments, and ignore the forgiveness He offers through Christ—will, tragically, end up there, too. Please be assured that this does not include babies or young children. Jesus is merciful, and God continues to protect the innocent. Yet our knowledge of the coming last battle, the end of time, and eternal rewards and punishments should cause us to remain on spiritual alert and to pray earnestly for those who do not yet know Jesus as Savior and Lord.

In study 19, we will examine some of the final events of the end of the age, including the last battle against Satan. While this subject could fill volumes, and believers have differences of opinion about the time lines of some events, the purpose of this study is to give an overview of the major themes and of essential spiritual truths that we can apply to our lives.

Memory Passage:

Then comes the end, when He delivers the kingdom to God the Father, when He puts an end to all rule and all authority and power. For He must reign till He has put all enemies under His feet. (1 Corinthians 15:24–25)

Study Questions

1. What will scoffers say in the last days about Jesus' promise to return to earth? (2 Peter 3:3–4)

   _____

   _____

2. Complete the following:

   2 Peter 3:8: *"With the Lord _____ _____ is as a thousand years, and a*

   _____ _____ as one day."

3. The apostle Peter wrote that God is not *"slack"* regarding the promise of Jesus' return. What, then, is the reason for the apparent delay? (2 Peter 3:9b, 15a NKJV, NIV)

   _____

   _____

4. What message of warning will God communicate to the people of the earth before the end of the age? (Revelation 14:6–7)

   _____

5. (a) Does any human being know the day or the hour when Jesus will return? (Matthew 24:36, 42; 25:13)

   _____

(b) How should we respond if people tell us that Christ has already returned to the earth and that they can even show us where He is? (Matthew 24:23, 26)

_____

(c) When Jesus and the apostle Peter described the manner in which the *"day of the Lord"* will occur, what vivid images did they compare it to?

Matthew 24:27: _____

2 Peter 3:10a: _____

6. When Christ returns, He will come *"on the clouds of heaven with* _____ *and*

_____ _____*"* (Matthew 24:30).

7. (a) How did the apostle Paul describe Jesus descending from heaven? (1 Thessalonians 4:16a)

_____

(b) Whom did he say would be resurrected first? (Verse 16b)

_____

(c) What will happen to the believers who are still alive at the time of Christ's coming? (Verse 17a)

_____

8. (a) Name various catastrophes and evils listed in Matthew 24 that Jesus said must come to pass on earth before He returns. [continued, next page]

Verses 6–7: _____

Verse 9: _____

Matthew 24:10: _____

Verse 11: _____

Verse 12: _____

(b) Who will be saved, even after experiencing these distressing conditions? (Verse 13)

_____

(c) What tremendous accomplishment will come to pass before Jesus returns? (Verse 14)

_____

9. Why do followers of Christ need to be discerning and watchful in the end times? (Matthew 24:24)

_____

10. What should believers do to prevent being deceived? (Matthew 24:42a; 25:13; 2 Peter 3:14b)

_____

_____

11. List two specific events connected to Satan's deception of the world that will occur before the coming of the Lord*. (2 Thessalonians 2:3)

(1) _____

(2) _____

12. The apostle Paul referred to the *"man of sin,"* who will come on the world scene at the end of the age, as the *"lawless one."* What will this lawless one do? (2 Thessalonians 2:4)

_____

_____

13. The apostle John called the lawless one the *"Antichrist."* He also wrote that *"many antichrists"*—that is, those who were like the Antichrist in nature—had surfaced and had gone out into the world *"from us"*—from the spiritual community of John and the believers he was writing to. (See 1 John 2:18–19a.) How did John explain that the believers could know that these antichrists had never been a true part of the church? (Verse 19b)

_____

_____

14. What does a person with the spirit of the Antichrist deny or refuse to confess?

1 John 2:22:_____

1 John 4:2–3: _____

15. (a) At the end of the age, what will Satan (the *"dragon"*) give to the first *"beast,"* who is a human instrument of his evil purposes? (Revelation 13:2b)

_____

(b) Whom will the people of the world worship? (Verses 4a, 8a)

_____

(c) What will people say about the beast? (Verse 4b)

_____

(d) Who will *not* worship the beast (the opposite of those mentioned in Revelation 13:8b)?

_____

16. (a) What will come out of the beast's mouth? (Revelation 13:6)

_____

(b) What will be granted to the beast? (Verse 7a)

_____

(c) The beast will also be given authority over what? (Verse 7b)

_____

17. Satan will also use a second "*beast*," or human instrument of evil, who will exercise the authority of the first beast. What are some things this second beast will do, according to Revelation 13?

Verse 13: _____

Verse 14: _____

_____

Verse 15: _____

_____

Verses 16–17: _____

_____

18. (a) Why will the spirits of demons perform signs for the kings of the earth—and the whole world? (Revelation 16:14b)

_____

(b) What is the name of the place where they will gather? (Verse 16)

_____

19. What will the Lamb (Jesus) do to those who make war against Him? (Revelation 17:14a)

_____

20. What three terms are used to describe the believers who are with the Lamb? (Verse 14b)

(1) _____ ; (2) _____ ;

(3) _____

21. Christ is depicted as riding on a white horse as He comes to defeat His enemies. How else is He described? (Revelation 19:12–13)

_____

22. (a) With what attribute will Christ judge and make war? (Revelation 19:11b)

_____

(b) What image is used for the weapon with which He will strike the rebellious nations? (Verse 15a)

_____

(c) What name will be written on Christ's robe and thigh? (Revelation 19:16)

_____

(d) Who will accompany Christ, riding on white horses? (Verse 14)

_____

23. When the beast, the kings of the earth, and their armies gather together to make war on Christ (see Revelation 19:19), what will happen to them?

(a) The beast (and the false prophet) will be… (Revelation 19:20)

_____

(b) The kings of the earth and their armies will be… (Verse 21)

_____

24. For what length of time will Satan be bound and prevented from deceiving people before his final attempt to overthrow God? (Revelation 20:2)

_____

25. Who will participate in the *"first resurrection"*—living and reigning with Christ? (Revelation 20:4)

_____

_____

26. After Satan is released from his imprisonment to deceive the nations one last time and to gather them for the final battle against God, what will happen…

(a) to the human armies? (Revelation 20:9)

_____

(b) to Satan? (Revelation 20:10)

_____

27. (a) God has appointed a final day when all human beings will be judged. Who will judge us? (Acts 10:42b; 17:31; 2 Timothy 4:1)

_____

(b) On what basis will we be judged? (2 Corinthians 5:10; Revelation 20:12b, 13b)

_____

28. By what will human beings who have rejected Jesus' words be judged? (John 12:48b)

_____

29. What will Jesus bring to light and reveal as He judges? (Romans 2:16; 1 Corinthians 4:5)

_____

_____

30. Whom will believers judge? (1 Corinthians 6:2–3)

(1) _____ ; (2) _____

31. What keys does Christ have? (Revelation 1:18)

_____

32. What and who will be cast into the lake of fire? (Revelation 20:14–15)

Verse 14: _____

Verse 15: _____

33. (a) Complete the following:

    1 Corinthians 15:25: *"Jesus must reign till He has put all* _____

    _____ _____ _____*."*

    (b) What will Jesus deliver to God the Father in the end? (Verse 24a)

_____

For Further Reflection

+ Read Psalm 145:8–9 and reread 2 Peter 3:8–9 (NKJV, NIV). In light of God's graciousness, compassion, goodness, tender mercies, and longsuffering (patience), think of someone or several people you can pray for today, that they may receive salvation through Christ.

+ As you contemplate the end of the age, remember that you can overcome Satan by the blood of the Lamb and by the word of your testimony—and by being willing to give your life, if necessary, for the sake of the gospel. (See Revelation 12:11.) Read, study, and meditate on the Word of God and look to it to sustain you at all times.

+ Since you do not know the day or hour when Jesus will return, endeavor each day to live as a faithful son or daughter of the King in love and obedience to Him.

When the War Is Over

Introduction

Imagine this: the last spiritual battle has been fought. Jesus has completely defeated Satan and his human instruments, and they never again will be able to accuse or attack those who have been redeemed by the Lamb of God. They will no longer be able to deceive and torment people. The war is over! Jesus has delivered the kingdom to God the Father—a kingdom of *"righteousness and peace and joy in the Holy Spirit"* (Romans 14:17). Daniel prophesied, *"His dominion is an everlasting dominion, which shall not pass away, and His kingdom the one which shall not be destroyed"* (Daniel 7:14).

Our final study in the *Spiritual Warfare Self-Study Bible Course* will be in two parts. Part 1, "A New Life," will explore what life will be like once we are no longer in spiritual warfare with Satan and his demons, and as we enter into the everlasting joy of our Lord*. (See Matthew 25:21, 23.) Part 2, "God Offers Us Eternal Life—How Will You Respond?" will review God's invitation to salvation for all who are thirsty for Him.

Memory Passage:

Who is this King of glory? The LORD strong and mighty, the LORD mighty in battle. Lift up your heads, O you gates! Lift up, you everlasting doors! And the King of glory shall come in. Who is this King of glory? The LORD of hosts, He is the King of glory. (Psalm 24:8–10)

Study Questions

Part I: A New Life

1. At the sound of the last trumpet, how will both the dead in Christ and the living in Christ be transformed? (1 Corinthians 15:52b–53)

   _____

   _____

2. (a) What does the Bible say will happen to creation on the day of the Lord? Complete the following:

   2 Peter 3:10b: *"The heavens will _____ _____ with a great noise, and the*

   elements will _____ with fervent heat; both the earth and the works that are in it

   will be _____ _____."

   (b) What has God promised will replace the old heavens and earth? (Verse 13)

   _____

   (c) Where will God then dwell? (Revelation 21:3)

   _____

3. (a) Whose face will we be able to see as we live on the new earth? (Revelation 22:4a)

   _____

   (b) What name will be on our foreheads? (Verse 4b)

   _____

(c) What did the apostle Paul explain would happen to him when he saw God face-to-face, something we, also, can anticipate happening to us? (1 Corinthians 13:12b)

_____

4. What did God say He would do in the new earth? (Revelation 21:5a)

_____

5. What *"former things"* will have passed away? (Revelation 21:4)

_____

6. The angel in Revelation told John that he would show him *"the bride, the Lamb's wife"* (Revelation 21:9), which is the body of Christ, or the church.

   (a) How is the church depicted in the new earth? (Revelation 21:10b–11a)

_____

   (b) How is the light of the church described? (Verse 11b)

_____

7. In the New Jerusalem, there will be a pure river of water of life, proceeding from the throne of God and the Lamb. (See Revelation 22:1.) Next to this river will be the tree of life.

   (a) What will this tree bear? (Revelation 22:2a)

_____

   (b) What are the leaves on the tree for? (Verse 2b)

_____

8. Why will those who dwell in the New Jerusalem no longer need any sun, moon, or lamp?

Revelation 21:23: _____

Revelation 22:5: _____

9. What statement did Jesus make about the nature of the righteous at the end of the age that corresponds to answer "b" in the previous question? (Matthew 13:43a)

_____

10. Describe the "materials" with which the New Jerusalem will be built, as depicted in Revelation 21:

   (1) The wall is _____. (Verse 18a)

   (2) The city is _____. (Verse 18b)

   (3) The foundations of the city wall are adorned with _____

   _____. (Verse 19a)

   (4) The twelve gates are _____

   _____. (Verse 21)

   (5) The street of the city is _____.
   (Verse 21b)

11. While He was on earth, Jesus often talked about the rewards that His followers would receive in heaven for obeying Him. (See, for example, Matthew 10:42; Mark 9:41; Luke 6:22–23, 35.) What overall term did the apostle Paul use to describe the reward we will receive for working as to the Lord* and not as to men? (Colossians 3:24)

_____

12. (a) In one of Jesus' parables about the kingdom of God, what did the King say to the "sheep" on His right hand—those who had genuinely served Him? Complete the following:

Matthew 25:34: *"Come, you* _____ *of My Father,*

_____ *the* _____ *prepared for you from the*

_____ *of the world."*

(b) When the "sheep" on His right hand protested that they had not directly ministered to Him, what assurance did the King give them? (Verse 40)

_____

_____

13. In another parable, what did the lord say to his obedient servants, which is a picture of what God will say to those whom He rewards? (Matthew 25:21, 23)

_____

_____

14. What has Jesus made us, in service to God the Father? (Revelation 1:6a; 5:10a)

_____

15. (a) Where will believers reign? (Revelation 5:10b)

_____

(b) For how long will they reign? (Revelation 22:5b)

_____

16. In what manner will believers be able to serve God, due to Jesus' final defeat of the devil? (Luke 1:74b–75)

_____

17. What did God say the one who overcomes will inherit? (Revelation 21:7a)

_____

18. What did God say about His relationship with the one who overcomes? (Verse 7b)

_____

Part II: God Offers Us Eternal Life—How Will You Respond?

19. (a) At the end of the book of Revelation, whom does John say will be blessed? (Revelation 22:14)

_____

(b) What will these blessed ones have a right to? (Verse 14a)

_____

(c) Where may they enter? (Verse 14b)

_____

20. What do the Spirit and the bride of Christ say to those who have not yet responded to God's offer of grace? (Revelation 22:17)

_____

21. Who may take of the water of life freely? (Revelation 22:17b)

_____

22. Who has the words of eternal life? (John 6:67–68)

_____

23. (a) What promise did Jesus give to those who hear His voice and follow Him? (John 10:27–28)

_____

(b) Who will receive eternal life? (John 3:16; Romans 2:7)

_____

24. What is eternal life? (John 17:3)

_____

25. How did Jesus say He is coming back to earth in power and glory? (Revelation 22:7a, 12a, 20)

_____

26. What should we do as we look forward to eternal life? (Jude 1:21)

_____

For Further Reflection

+ As you seek to serve God, (a) what are you doing for *"the least of these"* (Matthew 25:40)—those who need basic help in life, such as food, water, shelter, clothing, healing/medicine, and friendship? And (b) how are you using the gifts and calling God has given you to further His purposes and bring Him glory?

+ Are you still waiting to come to Jesus, through faith, and receive Him as Savior and Lord? If so, the Spirit and the bride (the church) are saying to you right now, "Come!" Are you thirsty for the water of life that Jesus alone can give you? Delay no longer. Pray the following prayer, which we first discussed at the end of study 3:

Heavenly Father, I come to You in the name of Your Son Jesus. I believe that You sent Him to earth to die for my sins and that You raised Him from the dead so that I might be completely forgiven and righteous in Him. Thank You for accepting me through Jesus, giving me eternal life, and welcoming me into Your family as Your own child. In Jesus' name, amen.

ANSWER KEY

Part I: The Realm of the Spirit

Study 1: God Is Spirit

1. God created the heavens and the earth; He made the world and everything in it.

2. God rules from His throne in heaven, or the "heavenly places."

3. God is described as "Spirit."

4. God is: (1) holiness*; (2) love

5. God is "invisible."

6. (1) eternal power; (2) Godhead*

7. (1) God the Father; (2) God the Son, Jesus Christ; (3) God the Spirit, or the Holy Spirit

8. All three persons of the Trinity participated in creation: God (the Father), the Spirit of God (Holy Spirit), and the Word (Jesus Christ, God's Son).

9. The image and likeness of God

10. (1) spirit; (2) soul*; (3) body

11. the spirit

12. (1) in spirit; (2) in truth

13. (1) visible; (2) invisible

14. God and that which is spiritual are greater than that which is earthly, or physical.

15. angels, sometimes referred to as the "host" of heaven

16. No. Angels are servants of God; they are not divine, and only God should be worshipped.

17. Angels minister on God's behalf to those who will inherit salvation (believers).

18. The invisible spiritual attributes of God's eternal power and Godhead* may be recognized and understood by human beings through the world He has created.

19. The tabernacle and religious practices given to the Israelites by God were "shadows" (foreshadows, hints) of what was later fulfilled through and in Jesus Christ; they were "copies" and "shadows" of heavenly things.

20. The Spirit of God* searches "all things," especially the deep things of God.

21. those who are led by the Spirit of God*

Study 2: Satan Declares War

1. God said all of His creation was *"very good."*

2. The Lord God came to the garden, where Adam and Eve lived, "in the cool of the day" (which apparently was a regular occurrence). He also called out to Adam, asking where he was.

3. (1) to have dominion over all the earth; (2) to be fruitful and multiply; (3) to fill the earth and subdue it

4. God commanded Adam not to eat of the tree of the knowledge of good and evil.

5. If Adam ate of the tree of the knowledge of good and evil, he would *"surely die."*

6. The serpent told Eve that she would not die if she ate the fruit from the tree of the knowledge of good and evil but that she would *"be like God, knowing good and evil."*

7. (1) They were made in God's image and likeness. (2) They exercised dominion, or ruled.

8. They disobeyed the command of God and ate fruit from the tree of the knowledge of good and evil.

9. Sin and death entered the world, and every person became subject to an eventual physical death; women experienced greater pain in childbirth; discord erupted between male and female, with the husband dominating the wife; the ground was cursed; work became toil; people had to grow their food rather than eat the fruit of the trees of the garden of Eden; human beings were banished from the garden of Eden.

10. No. Adam eventually died, and his body returned to the ground from which it had been created, just as God had said. Although the Bible doesn't specify Eve's death, it is implied as inevitable.

11. We have all sinned and fallen short of God's glory.

12. We are dead in our trespasses and sins, which is spiritual death (unless we are made alive in Christ).

13. the devil, or Satan

14. This spiritual being was once called Lucifer; his name and description, *"son of the morning,"* indicate light, or goodness.

15. Lucifer was *"the anointed cherub who covers,"* or an angelic being, created and established by God.

16. Lucifer wanted to be exalted to God's level and be like Him, because he was vain, prideful, and power hungry.

17. Jesus called Satan the *"evil one"* and *"wicked one,"* as well as a *"murderer,"* a *"liar"* in whom there is *"no truth,"* *"the father of lies,"* and *"the thief"* who comes to steal, kill, and destroy.

18. *"the ruler of this world"*

19. All of creation was also subjected to bondage when Adam and Eve disobeyed God.

20. Yes, Satan can operate only as far as God allows; he was expelled from heaven, and he is answerable to God and judged for his rebellion.

21. God is always the world's ultimate Owner and Ruler; He is *"the Possessor of heaven and earth."*

22. Events/problems that occur on earth can have a spiritual origin, and what happens in one realm (heaven or earth) can affect the other.

23. Satan transforms himself into an *"angel of light"* in order to deceive people into believing that what he suggests or does is good, when it is actually destructive, and he uses various people as his *"ministers"* or *"servants"* (NIV) in the same way.

24. Satan also enlists the following to carry out his evil work on earth: demons, also called evil spirits or deceiving spirits; principalities; powers; rulers of the darkness of this age; spiritual hosts of wickedness in the heavenly places.

25. Demons were once angels who joined Satan in rebelling against God (apparently a third of God's angels) and were cast out of heaven.

26. Satan causes illness, disease, and demon possession; incites people to do wrong; steals the Word of God from people's hearts; mixes the false with the genuine in order to deceive people; oppresses people; works *"wiles"* (*"schemes"* NIV) against people; takes people captive to do his will; causes people trials, such as imprisonment, as well as tribulation; causes death; causes destruction on the earth out of his wrath.

27. God will deliver us from every evil work of Satan and preserve us for His heavenly kingdom.

28. Yes, God desires to live within us and to fellowship with us.

Study 3: Renewed by the Spirit

1. Humanity's nature was that of being spiritually dead in trespasses and sins; following the corrupt desires of the flesh* and mind; *"children of wrath"*; unrighteous; lacking in understanding; failing to seek God; and no longer living in God's glory.

2. Sin and Satan control those who have a spiritually dead nature.

3. sexual immorality, impurity, debauchery, idolatry, witchcraft, hatred, discord, jealousy, fits of rage, selfish ambition, dissensions, factions and envy, drunkenness, and orgies

4. Because of His love for us, God forgave us of our sins and made us spiritually alive again through His Son Jesus, who took the punishment we deserved for our sin. As we believe in Jesus, we receive eternal life.

5. We confess Jesus as Lord and believe in our hearts that God has raised Him from the dead.

6. Jesus' death and resurrection freed us from the bondage of the devil and the fear of death. Jesus has delivered us from the power of darkness, so that we now live in His kingdom.

7. We become a new creation; the old nature is gone, we are freed from sin and its control, and we can live according to the resurrection life of Jesus.

8. No. Jesus Christ is our only means to salvation and freedom from sin.

9. We received the Holy Spirit, who is the Spirit of God and of Christ. He is the Spirit of Truth, our Helper, who dwells in us and with us forever. He is the *"Spirit of adoption"* in that we become God's children when He indwells us.

10. life

11. (a) No, our bodies are still "dead." (b) Our bodies will be given life through the Spirit, with the same incorruptible and immortal resurrection body that Jesus has.

12. God becomes our Father.

13. We become God's children through a spiritual rebirth. We are His heirs and joint heirs with Jesus Christ.

14. We are able to draw near to God, and we have access to His throne of grace.

15. Paul struggled with not always practicing the godly things he wanted to do but instead doing the ungodly things he did *not* want to do. He delighted in the law of God in his *"inward man,"* but the sinful nature warred against him, sometimes making him "captive" to the law of sin.

16. (1) the lust of the flesh*; (2) the lust of the eyes; (3) the pride of life

17. We overcome Satan's attacks when he uses our sinful flesh* by recognizing that there is no condemnation to those who are in Christ Jesus when they live and walk according to the Spirit, according to the law of the Spirit of life in Christ Jesus, which has freed us from the law of sin and death. When we are spiritually minded, we have life and peace.

18. The fruit (nature) of the Spirit is love, joy, peace, longsuffering, kindness, goodness, faithfulness, gentleness, and self-control.

19. God is able to strengthen us with might through His Spirit in the inner man, so that Christ may dwell in our hearts through faith, and so that we, being rooted and grounded in love, may be able to comprehend the width, length, depth, and height of the love of Christ, which is beyond human knowledge, and so that we may be filled with all the fullness of God. He is able to do exceedingly abundantly above all that we ask or think, according to the power that works in us.

20. The Holy Spirit sanctifies us.

21. We cooperate in the process of sanctification* by presenting ourselves to God as a "living sacrifice," holy and acceptable to Him, and by being transformed by the renewing of our minds as we come to learn the good, acceptable, and perfect will of God; by seeking godly things as we set our minds on things in heaven, not on things on the earth; by rejecting the fallen nature, with its deceitful lusts, including such things as fornication, uncleanness, passion, evil desire, covetousness, anger, wrath, malice, blasphemy, filthy language, and lying; by "putting on" the new nature, which is God's nature of true righteousness and holiness*.

22. God has sent us His Spirit, so that He can reveal Himself and what He has freely given to us, because these things are spiritually discerned.

23. We can renew our minds to conform to God's ways by reading, being convicted by, and obeying His Word, as well as by asking God to keep us from sin and to let our thoughts and words be honorable to Him.

24. (a) "death"; (b) being spiritually minded

25. We should confess our sins to God and receive His forgiveness through Christ, who paid the price on the cross for our sins.

26. (a) the ministry of reconciliation; (b) Christ; world; trespasses; (c) ambassadors for Christ

Study 4: What Spiritual Warfare Is All About

1. (1) the kingdom of God, which is Jesus' kingdom; (2) the kingdom of Satan, or the *"power of darkness"*

2. Jesus' realm is good. Through it, He brings abundant, eternal life and frees people from spiritual, emotional, and physical enslavement. Satan's domain is evil. Through it, he brings loss, death, and destruction and binds people up in oppression.

3. Several aspects of God's nature are His holiness*, His love, His eternal power, and His Godhead*.

4. (1) righteousness; (2) peace; (3) joy

5. Satan is a murderer, liar, thief, wicked one who snatches the truth of God from people, and deceiver.

6. power of darkness, principalities; rulers of the darkness of this age, spiritual hosts of wickedness in the heavenly places

7. These visions indicate God's overwhelming holiness* and omnipotence, as well as His grace toward human beings.

8. Satan tried to tempt Jesus to: (1) Command stones to become bread, to feed His human appetite. (2) Throw Himself down from the pinnacle of the temple, as a test for God to rescue Him. (3) Bow down and worship Satan, a violation of the greatest commandment to love God and worship Him alone.

9. Satan wants all peoples on earth to worship and serve him.

10. lies/falsehoods and deception

11. The image and likeness of God within human beings become corrupted, leading to sin and various forms of depraved thinking. People become filled with every kind of wickedness, evil, greed, depravity, envy, murder, strife, deceit, and malice. They become gossips, slanderers, God-haters, insolent, arrogant, and boastful; they invent ways of doing evil; they disobey their parents; they become senseless, faithless, heartless, and ruthless. Ignoring the consequences of their behavior, some people not only continue to do these very things but also approve of those who practiced them.

12. By relying on the *"anointing"*—by allowing the Holy Spirit within us to teach us God's truth and by obeying that truth, abiding in Jesus Christ.

13. *"the accuser of our brethren* [believers]"

14. We can protect ourselves against Satan's accusations by recognizing that since we are in Christ Jesus and walk according to the Spirit, we are no longer under the condemnation of sin. If we do sin, we have an Advocate with the Father, Jesus Christ the righteous, who is the propitiation for our sins.

15. Jesus disarmed them, making a public spectacle of them and triumphing over them in it.

16. Jesus gives believers power and authority over all the power of the enemy, including demons, as well as power and authority to cure diseases and to heal other sicknesses.

17. the kingdom of God

18. Satan has already been cast out of heaven, and believers overcome him through the blood of the Lamb and the word of their testimony. Satan is under God's control and will inevitably be cast into the lake of fire forever. Jesus destroyed Satan through His death on the cross, and He has disarmed the principalities and powers of darkness.

19. the Lord Jesus Christ

20. God's love for us, which is in Christ Jesus our Lord

21. (a) establishes; has anointed; sealed; given us the Spirit (b) sanctify*; preserved blameless; (c) Paul said that God who called them is faithful, and He would do it

22. to be with us always, even to the end of the age

Part II: A Global War/A Personal War

Study 5: Enlisted in God's Army

1. endure hardship and be a good soldier of Jesus Christ

2. Jesus expects believers to exercise their power over all the power of the enemy and to heal the sick and diseased, raise the dead, and cast out demons.

3. to freely share our kingdom benefits with other people, breaking Satan's bondage over them; to show that we belong to Jesus by working for Him, rather than against Him; to glorify God through His Son Jesus

4. watch out for the schemes and attacks of the enemy; stand fast in our faith; remain in the freedom Christ has given us and not allow Satan to bring us back under his oppression; be brave; be strong; maintain love for our fellow believers and those who do not yet know the Lord

5. We must remain focused on the spiritual war in which we are engaged, not allowing ourselves to be distracted by less important things, and we must continue to be obedient to God, following His ways and instructions to us.

6. We are to stand fast with other believers with one spirit and mind, share God's love, practice humility by looking out for the interests of others, strive together for the faith of the gospel, not fear those who oppose the gospel, and avoid complaints and disputes, so that we can be a witness to the world of the truth of Christ.

7. God gives us His Holy Spirit, the Spirit of Truth, to be our Helper; He is active in us so that we both desire to do His will and endeavor to carry it out; He works in us what is well pleasing in His sight, through Jesus Christ, making us complete in every good work to do His will

8. Satan

9. the human being who has been redeemed (because of Christ who lives within him)

10. (1) Submit to God. (2) Resist the devil.

11. Our weapons are *"mighty in God for pulling down strongholds."* They are not *"carnal,"* or the kind of verbal or physical weapons people use against other people in the world.

12. truth, with which we "gird" our waists; the breastplate of righteousness; the "shoes" of the preparation of the gospel of peace; the shield of faith; the helmet of salvation; and the sword of the Spirit, which is the Word of God

13. the whole armor

14. the Lord God

15. They subdued kingdoms, worked righteousness, obtained promises, stopped the mouths of lions, quenched the violence of fire, escaped the edge of the sword, out of weakness were made strong, became valiant in battle, and turned to flight the armies of the aliens (foreign armies).

16. Our strength comes from the Lord* and the power of His might, because Christ gives us the strength to do all things.

17. (1) by the blood of the Lamb (Jesus); (2) by the word of their testimony; (3) by not loving their lives to the death

18. (1) establish us; (2) guard us from the evil one (the devil)

Study 6: The Stakes Are High

1. (1) the ruler of this world; (2) the god of this age

2. the sway of the wicked one

3. It is characterized as evil.

4. (1) steal; (2) kill; (3) destroy

5. Jesus came to save the world, to bring abundant life to people, and to destroy the works of the devil.

6. (1) everlasting life/the resurrection of life; (2) everlasting contempt and shame/the resurrection of condemnation

7. No. Everyone who has ever lived will be judged.

8. nations and people who did not turn away from evil to follow God; anyone not found in the Book of Life—those who never knew God in relationship or lived according to His ways

9. the Lord God of heaven

10. (1) the earth will be filled with the knowledge of the glory of the Lord*; (2) God's kingdom will come and His purposes will be accomplished on earth as they are in heaven; (3) the kingdoms of this world will become God's kingdoms and those of Christ, and He will reign over the earth forever

11. (a) God is longsuffering toward those who are under Satan's control and are living according to the sinful nature. He is not willing that any should perish (be eternally condemned) but that all should come to repentance (receive eternal life). (b) God desires to "pluck them from the fire," or rescue them from eternal death, by clothing them in the righteousness of Christ.

12. Before we were saved, we were "dead" in trespasses and sins–we walked according to the course of this world, according to the prince of the power of the air (Satan), who works in the sons of disobedience, conducting ourselves in the lusts of our flesh*, fulfilling the desires of the flesh* and of the mind. We were by nature children of wrath.

13. God saved us and made us spiritually alive through our faith, as a gift to us. Through His grace and kindness in Christ Jesus, He has raised us up and caused us to sit in the heavenly places in Christ.

14. Satan causes his demons to possess people and try to destroy them.

15. Demons recognized that Jesus was the *"Holy One of God"* or the *"Son of the Most High God"*—the Messiah, God's own Son, whom God had sent to free people from Satan's power. They recognized that He had the power to command them to leave the people they were tormenting and to go back into hell, and that He would destroy them.

16. The demons recognized that their time to torment human beings was limited—it would come to an end, and they would be eternally punished.

17. to bring abundant life to people; to preach the gospel to the poor; to heal the broken-hearted; to proclaim liberty to the captives and recovery of sight to the blind; to set at liberty those who are oppressed; to seek and to save those who are lost.

18. Jesus cast out demons; healed the sick, including the blind, the deaf, and the lame; He cleansed the lepers and raised the dead; He preached the gospel to the poor; He sought and saved those who were lost, such as Zacchaeus.

19. to His disciples, and, through them, to all who would believe in Him in all times

20. They went out and preached the gospel everywhere, the Lord* working with them and confirming God's Word through accompanying signs; they brought salvation to the lost; they healed the sick and lame; they did signs and wonders; and they cast out demons.

21. those who abide in Jesus and His Word and who have Jesus' words abiding in them, so that they bear much spiritual fruit; those who have genuine love for their fellow believers; and those who do the will of God the Father.

22. We should be keeping Jesus' commandments; doing the good works that God prepared beforehand that we should "walk" in; praying that God would send laborers out into the "harvest" of the world to preach the gospel of the kingdom and to heal and deliver people; engaging in the same works that Jesus did when He was on earth, and even "greater" works.

23. Jesus prayed for all believers, asking God the Father to keep us through His name, protect us from the evil one, and sanctify* us by His truth; God is able to keep us from stumbling and to present us faultless before Him.

Study 7: Satan's Strategies and Attacks, Part 1

1. Satan is sometimes referred to as the *"prince of the power of the air."* We can infer from this name that Satan operates from the spiritual atmosphere, or realm, around us, including certain domains in the heavens above the earth

2. (1) principalities; (2) powers; (3) the rulers of the darkness of this age; (4) spiritual hosts of wickedness in the heavenly places

3. *New King James Version:* "wiles"; *New International Version:* "schemes"

4. We should be sober and vigilant to recognize ways in which the devil may try to deceive or destroy us, and we should resist the enemy, remaining steadfast in the faith.

5. an angel of light (truth)

6. (1) If we doubt in our hearts, we lose our spiritual power and miss out on answered prayer. (2) Since anything we do that is not based on faith is sin, an undermining of our faith will likely lead us to sin.

7. the entirety of God's Word is truth, and it endures forever; Jesus is the Word of God, and He brought grace, truth, and light to us from the Father; God's Word is not as the word of men but is truly the Word of God that effectively works in us who believe; only through faith can we please God.

8. through false prophets, deceiving spirits, doctrines of demons, and blinding people's minds to the truth

9. 1 John 4:1: We are not to believe every person or teaching that claims to have the truth from God, but we are to *"test the spirits"* to see whether they come from Him.

   Matthew 7:16–20: We are to look at the "fruit" of people's lives who claim to have the truth and see if it corresponds to God's nature and ways.

10. They would no longer be influenced by every "wind" of doctrine or be deceived by people's cunningness and craftiness

11. Jesus recognized that Satan was taking God's Word out of context. He responded with Scripture that revealed God's truth in relation to Satan's attempted deception.

12. false signs and wonders

13. Again, the way to discern false signs and wonders is to see if they and the people performing them exhibit the "fruit" of God—His nature and character. If people truly know God, they will love Him, obey His commands, and exhibit His love and self-sacrificing nature. They will not just try to dazzle and overwhelm people with their feats. God's signs and wonders always support His gospel of salvation through Jesus Christ.

14. (a) No. God cannot be tempted by evil, and neither does He tempt anyone else. (b) We are tempted when we are drawn away from what is right and good by our own evil desires, and enticed. (c) sin; (d) death

15. gluttony; revelry ["*orgies*" NIV]; drunkenness; lewdness; strife; envy/covetousness; fulfilling the lust of the flesh*, the lust of the eyes, and the pride of life/fulfilling the desires of the flesh* and of the mind (without Christ); violence; greed for money; quarrelsomeness; idolatry

16. Some people forsake God's truth through their covetousness and the lusts of their flesh*; they are deceived by the pursuit of their own carnal desires. Some of them entice others who are not spiritually stable to do the same, through the lusts of their flesh*, bringing these others back into bondage to Satan, also, by way of *"swelling words of emptiness,"* or false teaching.

17. We are assured that God will not allow us to be tempted beyond what we are able to withstand but will make a way of escape for us, so that we will be able to bear it. We

are also assured that when we submit to God and resist the devil, he will flee from us, removing the source of temptation.

18. Jesus was victorious over the devil's temptations through the Word of God, and we can respond in the same way. Jesus sympathizes with our struggles because He was tempted in all the same ways that we are while He lived on earth. However, He never sinned, and He is now our High Priest or Mediator in heaven. Therefore, when we struggle with temptation, we can go to Him and receive His strength and help to overcome it.

19. No, the devil just waited until an *"opportune time"* to tempt Him again.

20. Be watchful for temptations and pray for strength; walk in the Spirit and be led by Him; put to death the misdeeds of the body through the Spirit; crucify the passions and desires of the flesh* and reign over sin through Christ; "put off" the old nature and "put on" Christ and His righteous nature, making no provision for the flesh*; exercise self-discipline; be content with what we have; set our minds on things above, not on things on the earth; don't dwell on the temptation but meditate on what is true, noble, just, pure, lovely, of good report, virtuous, and praiseworthy.

21. If we "sow" to our flesh*, or indulge in carnal desires, we will "reap" corruption, but if we "sow" to the Spirit, walking in the ways of God, we will "reap" everlasting life.

22. by denying Christ; by sinning in not doing what we should do or doing what we shouldn't do; by spoiling our Christian testimony in front of those who are outside the faith through our attitudes and/or behavior

23. confess our sins to God and receive His forgiveness and cleansing; ask other people for forgiveness, as applicable; confess our sins to one another; endeavor to lay aside the sin that so easily ensnares us, running with endurance the spiritual race before us

24. loves

25. Romans 8:1: We have no condemnation; we walk according to the Spirit.

   2 Corinthians 5:17a, 18a: We are new creations in Christ; we are reconciled to God.

Study 8: Satan's Strategies and Attacks, Part 2

26. He told them not to sin in their anger and not to let their anger go unresolved, for in doing so, they would *"give place"* (NKJV) to the devil, or allow him to get a *"foothold"* (NIV), in their lives.

27. by disbelieving God and rebelling against Him (rebellion is like the sin of witchcraft); by complaining and blaming God for their situations; by succumbing to discouragement and fear; by stubbornly resisting what is right; by rejecting God's Word; by refusing to forgive others and becoming bitter; by sharing in other people's sins; by envying

evil men, especially when they grow rich; by being spiritually lukewarm; by being self-reliant and living as if they don't need God

28. by believing God and trusting Him completely; by leaning on His understanding and not our own; by acknowledging God in all our ways; by forgiving others; by replacing our fear with power, love, and a sound mind from the Holy Spirit

29. *Job*: Job did not sin when provoked by Satan because he continued to trust God and worship Him, and he did not accuse God of wrongdoing.

    David: David's action was sinful because, as Joab essentially told him, all of Israel's soldiers belonged to God, so the battles they would face would be the Lord's to win, and He would fight for them. David should have understood that he shouldn't look to human strength but instead should go to God for help. As was the case with Gideon and his fighting men in Judges 7, God wanted the Israelites to know that He alone was their Savior and Protector.

    Judas Iscariot: At least one of the reasons Judas arrived at his dire spiritual state was that he allowed sin in his life; he was greedy and a habitual thief, opening the door to Satan's influence. Judas cared more about riches than about God's righteousness, truth, and loyalty, and he was destroyed for it.

    Ananias and Sapphira: This husband and wife lied to God and agreed together to "test" the Holy Spirit, and they died for their deception, apparently as an example, to keep such attitudes and behavior from spreading in the fledgling church.

30. (a) the tongue; (b) tongue; world of iniquity; defiles the whole body; the course of nature; (c) by being swift to hear, slow to speak, and slow to wrath; by letting no corrupt word proceed out of our mouths but instead speaking only what is good and what will edify others; by not lashing out at others when we are angry but instead being quiet before the Lord*, putting our trust in Him regarding the situation

31. by living a life of love; by continually rejoicing in God, praying without ceasing, and giving thanks to Him in everything

32. (a) The devil takes away God's Word from people's hearts, so that they will not believe and be saved. (b) People can prevent this from happening by having an open heart to hear God's Word and by being willing to obey it, so that the Word remains inside them, and they bear fruit over time.

33. Jesus said that the woman with the spirit of infirmity that caused her to be bent over had been bound by Satan for eighteen years; Jesus healed all who were oppressed by the devil.

34. (a) He must be bound. (b) Jesus gave His followers the "keys" of the kingdom of heaven, so that whatever they bind on earth will be bound in heaven, and whatever they loose on earth will be loosed in heaven. (c) In essence, if Christ and the Holy Spirit are not living within a formerly demon-possessed person to fill and protect him and enable him to walk according to the Spirit, then he is not permanently delivered; he is vulnerable to being possessed by demons again, in an even worse way.

35. No, because Jesus said that His followers would be persecuted, and the apostle Paul wrote that everyone who wants to live a godly life in Christ will suffer persecution.

36. Jesus said those who are persecuted for their faith in Him—who are reviled, persecuted, and falsely accused of all kinds of evil—are blessed; they will receive the kingdom of heaven and great reward.

37. (a) Because persecution is a partaking of Christ's sufferings, and if we experience some of His sufferings, we will also share in His joy when His glory is revealed; and because, when we are reproached for the name of Christ, the Spirit of glory and of God rests upon us. (b) Some people may suffer reproach or punishment not because of persecution but because they committed a wrong, such as murdering, stealing, or being an evildoer or a busybody.

38. They fall away from the faith.

39. by loving our enemies; by blessing those who curse us (rather than cursing back) and who persecute us; by doing good to those who hate us; by praying for those who spitefully use us and persecute us; by being "*wise as serpents* [discerning, watchful, not putting our ultimate trust in people] *and harmless as doves* [pure in heart, righteous, filled with God's love]" in dealing with people; by not worrying about how or what we should speak when we are brought before officials and asked to give an account of our faith, because the Holy Spirit will give us the words to say; by not giving up, and enduring persecution to the end; by rejoicing in tribulations, recognizing that they produce perseverance in us, which leads to the building of our character and, ultimately, a strong hope (confident expectation) in God; by appreciating even infirmities, reproaches, needs, persecutions, and distresses that we experience for Christ's sake, because God displays His strength through our weakness; by exercising patience and faith; by committing ourselves to our faithful Creator* and doing what is good; by allowing ourselves to learn and grow spiritually through persecution, so that it can produce the peaceable fruit of righteousness in us.

40. Because it was the Father's will in conjunction with carrying out His plan of redemption for human beings, and because the Father allowed the "*power of darkness*" (Satan) to cause it to come about for this purpose.

41. the opportunity for Christians who have been detained/arrested to testify to their faith in Jesus to the officials holding them; an increase in the spread of the gospel when Christians are scattered due to the persecution, and they preach the Word of God in regions they wouldn't have gone into otherwise, giving more people an occasion to hear and respond

42. (1) virtue; (2) knowledge; (3) self-control; (4) perseverance; (5) godliness; (6) brotherly kindness; (7) love

43. our Lord Jesus Christ

Part III: Enabling Our Warfare

Study 9: The Holy Spirit: Comforter, Helper, and Guide

1. They would be baptized with the Holy Spirit.

2. (a) power; (b) to enable them to be witnesses for Jesus in Jerusalem, Judea, Samaria, and to the end of the earth

3. (a) a rushing mighty wind; (b) divided "tongues," like fire, which came upon each of Jesus' followers

4. They began to speak with other tongues, as the Spirit gave them utterance.

5. three thousand

6. Acts 4:31, 33a: The place where the believers were assembled was shaken; the believers were filled with the Holy Spirit, and they spoke the Word of God with boldness; the apostles witnessed to the resurrection of the Lord Jesus with great power.

   Acts 5:12a: Many signs and wonders were done among the people through the apostles.

7. (a) the Holy Spirit; (b) fallen upon none of them

8. *New King James Version*: "Helper"; *King James Version*: "Comforter"; *New International Version*: "Counselor"

9. The Holy Spirit would teach them *"all things,"* and He would bring to their remembrance everything that Jesus had said to them.

10. By enabling us to remember and understand Jesus' teachings, the Holy Spirit helps us to better know how to respond with God's Word to the devil's temptations.

11. The Holy Spirit guides us into all truth; He tells us about things to come; He takes of Jesus (and the Father) and declares it to us; He reveals what has been freely given to us by God.

12. (1) wisdom; understanding; (2) counsel; might; (3) knowledge; (4) the fear of the Lord*

13. The Spirit makes intercession for us, according to the will of God, with groanings that cannot be uttered.

14. The Spirit has "moved upon" them or "moved" their spirits, "stirred up" their spirits, or "compelled" them, so that they acted in accordance with His will, thereby accomplishing His purposes.

15. (1) love; (2) joy; (3) peace; (4) longsuffering; (5) kindness; (6) goodness; (7) faithfulness; (8) gentleness; (9) self-control

16. love our enemies, bless those who curse us, do good to those who hate us, and pray for those who spitefully use us and persecute us

17. "Overcome evil with good."

18. Luke 22:47–51: Jesus showed compassion to one of His enemies. When Peter cut off the ear of the servant of the high priest, who had come with the religious officials and soldiers to arrest Jesus, Jesus made the ear whole again.

   Luke 23:33–34: Jesus forgave those who crucified Him because they did not realize what they were doing.

19. fear of the Lord*; comfort of the Holy Spirit; multiplied

Study 10: The Holy Spirit's Gifts

1. (1) apostle; (2) prophet; (3) evangelist; (4) pastor; (5) teacher

2. (1) the word of wisdom; (2) the word of knowledge; (3) faith; (4) gifts of healings; (5) the working of miracles; (6) prophecy; (7) discerning of spirits; (8) different kinds of tongues; (9) the interpretation of tongues

3. No. Each believer is given a particular manifestation of the Holy Spirit, according to the Spirit's will, "*for the profit of all.*" Each gift fulfills a particular function that is needed in the body of Christ.

4. (a) The Holy Spirit guided Philip and gave him wisdom and discernment to explain the gospel to the Ethiopian official who was reading a prophecy about Jesus from the book of Isaiah. (b) After Paul and Silas were blocked by the Holy Spirit from going in certain directions to share the gospel, Paul received a vision in the night by the Holy Spirit, from which they concluded that the Lord* wanted them to bring the gospel to Macedonia. Later, Paul received knowledge from the Spirit that he was to go to Jerusalem and then Rome.

5. The Spirit gives us wisdom about the way we should proceed in life; He guides us into all truth; if we lack wisdom, we can ask God for it, and He will give it to us, as long as we ask in faith.

6. He did great wonders and signs among the people.

7. Jesus healed all kinds of sickness and all kinds of disease among the people. There was no sickness or disease He was not able to cure.

8. Philip did miracles and signs in Samaria, in conjunction with his preaching of the gospel. Among the miracles he performed were casting demons out of many people and healing many who were paralyzed and lame. Paul (and Barnabas) did many miracles and wonders among the Gentiles. God also worked unusual miracles through Paul, so that even handkerchiefs or aprons that were brought from his body to those who were sick caused the diseases and the evil spirits to leave them.

9. The Holy Spirit used a prophet named Agabus from Judea to prophecy to Paul about how he would be bound by the Jews in Jerusalem and be delivered into the hands of the Gentiles.

10. *Discernment of the Human Spirit*: Acts 5:1–11: Peter discerned that Ananias and Sapphira were lying. Acts 14:8–10: Paul discerned that the man in Lystra had the faith to be healed, even though the man had been crippled since birth.

    Discernment of Angelic Beings: Matthew 1:20–25: Joseph discerned an angel speaking to him in a dream and learned that he should take Mary as His wife and that he should give her unborn son, who had been conceived by the Holy Spirit, the name Jesus. Acts 5:17–25: The apostles saw the angel of the Lord, who delivered them from prison and directed them to preach the gospel in the temple.

    Discernment of Demonic Influence and Entities: Acts 13:6–12: Paul, *"filled with the Holy Spirit"* and examining Elymas intently, discerned that Elymas was a sorcerer and a false prophet who was operating out of satanic influence. Acts 16:16–18: Even though the slave girl was proclaiming truthful things about Paul and his companions, Paul discerned that she had a spirit of divination, and he commanded the evil spirit to come out of her.

11. (1) tongues of men; (2) tongues of angels

12. The apostle Paul said he wished all the Corinthian believers spoke in tongues, indicating that this general gift of tongues is available to everyone in the body of Christ.

13. It translates a message in tongues so that the words spoken may edify the church.

14. Paul instructed that a person who has a message in tongues should pray to God for the interpretation. He also said that only two or three people should speak in tongues in a

gathering of believers, each should speak in turn, and one should interpret, so that the tongues are spoken in an orderly way that benefits the people. Also, if no interpreter is present (or if the person with the gift of tongues did not receive the interpretation), the believer with the message in tongues must keep silent and speak only to himself and to God.

15. They confirm to unbelievers the truth of the message of the gospel of Jesus Christ that has been presented to them.

16. (1) visions; (2) dreams

17. To direct Ananias to minister to Saul (Paul), to reassure him about this assignment, and to give him knowledge and instruction to convey to Paul regarding his God-given calling to bring the gospel to Jews, Gentiles, and kings.

18. To confirm that the gospel of salvation in Jesus Christ and the gift of the Holy Spirit were for the Gentiles, as well as for the Jews.

19. Genesis 41: God gave a supernatural dream to the Egyptian pharaoh and the interpretation of the dream to Joseph not only to promote and bless Joseph, but also as a warning about an impending national crisis and how the nation could prepare for it, so that the people of Egypt and surrounding countries and regions (including Joseph's family) could survive.

   Matthew 2:7–15: God gave supernatural dreams to the wise men and Joseph in order to protect the newborn Jesus from death at the hands of Herod.

20. revelation

21. the spirit (or Spirit) of wisdom and revelation in the knowledge of Him

Study 11: Angels: God's Servants on Our Behalf

1. Angels heed God's voice and perform His Word. They minister on God's behalf and are sent by God to minister to those who will inherit salvation (who have received Jesus).

2. No. Angel worship is false teaching. Angels are our "fellow servants"; God alone is to be worshipped.

3. Angels "excel in strength" and can be very powerful, but they are not all-powerful, as God is. At times, they need other angels to help them fight against potent demonic forces.

4. They worship, honor, and bless Him.

5. (a) Jesus is higher than angels and has a greater name than they do. He is God's own Son, who sits at God's right hand, while angels are God's servants. Jesus is God Himself, and He is worshipped by the angels. Angels, authorities, and powers are subject to Him.
   (b) This statement refers to Jesus humbling Himself and becoming a Man to die on the

Answer Key 201

cross to save us from our sins, after which God highly exalted Him and gave Him the name that is above all names (including angels). Jesus has all authority in heaven and on earth and is crowned with glory and honor.

6. as an "innumerable company"

7. heaven and earth

8. (1) seraphim; (2) cherubim

9. archangel

10. the Lord*

11. They sometimes work alone (apparently) and sometimes work with other angels.

12. The angel of the Lord stood in front of Balaam and the donkey he was riding, with his sword in his hand, blocking their way three different times. At first, the donkey alone saw the angel, and the animal reacted by stopping (and was struck by Balaam). After the third time, the Lord* opened Balaam's eyes to see the angel, and He told the prophet to speak only the word He told him, and Balaam was obedient.

13. (a) The angel was standing between earth and heaven, and in his hand was a drawn sword stretched out over Jerusalem. (b) They fell on their faces. (c) He returned his sword to its sheath.

14. They ministered to Him and strengthened Him.

15. (1) guard/protect/defend; (2) rescue/deliver; (3) bring information/instruction/guidance/encouragement/revelation from God; (4) aid in receiving and understanding revelation from the Lord*; (5) strengthen/sustain; (6) offer believers' prayers with incense before God; (7) escort believers to heaven when they die

16. (a) fear/terror/unease; (b) The angels told them not to be afraid and gave them reassuring and encouraging news.

17. when we show hospitality to strangers, since angels can disguise themselves as human beings

18. They are joyful.

19. keep them along the way and bring them into the place that God had prepared for them

20. Genesis 32:1–2: Angels are referred to as an encamped army.

Joshua 5:14: A powerful angel (or perhaps a pre-incarnate appearance by Jesus) informed Joshua that he was the "commander of the army of the Lord."

21. (a) horses and chariots of fire; (b) one hundred and eighty-five thousand

22. All of God's angels will accompany Christ in His return; with a *"great sound of a trumpet,"* they will gather together all the elect (believers); they will exhibit the glory that God gave them.

23. The angels will witness Jesus confessing or denying people before them, based on whether those people confessed Him or denied Him while they were on earth.

Part IV: The Weapons of Our Warfare

Study 12: The Whole Armor of God, Part 1

1. God's armor

2. rock (as in strategic position), fortress, deliverer, shield, horn, stronghold

3. (a) "put on" the whole armor of God; (b) "take up" the whole armor of God

4. (a) truth (with which we "gird" our waists); (b) the belt of truth

5. Jesus Christ

6. (1) by abiding in Jesus' word, or teaching; (2) by being guided by the Spirit of truth (Holy Spirit)

7. to sanctify* us by His truth, or His Word

8. in our *"inward parts"* (NKJV), or *"innermost being"* (NASB)

9. (1) they are self-seeking; (2) they are deceived or in denial about the sin in their life

10. if we love by our actions and in truth, not just by what we say

11. the truth

12. the breastplate of righteousness

13. (a) God's; (b) Jesus Christ

14. (a) our own righteousness; (b) because our "righteousness" is like filthy rags, still containing iniquity

15. because the heart is highly deceitful and *"desperately"* wicked

16. the heart

17. pure

18. by confessing our sins to God and receiving His forgiveness

19. all of Scripture

20. the chastening, or discipline, of God in our lives

21. (a) as instruments of unrighteousness to sin; (b) (1) ourselves; (2) the members of our bodies

22. our *"new man"*

23. dead; alive; Christ Jesus our Lord

24. (spiritual) fruits

25. *"No weapon formed against you shall prosper, and every tongue which rises against you in judgment you shall condemn."*

26. (a) the preparation of the gospel of peace; (b) shoes

27. peace and goodwill

28. (a) by being justified by faith, through Jesus Christ; (b) the blood of Jesus, which He shed through His death on the cross

29. He reconciled them to God through *one* body (His body, which died on the cross) and gave them access to God the Father through *one* Spirit.

30. (a) peace, or His peace; (b) the kind of peace the world gives

31. (a) It will guard our hearts and minds through Christ Jesus. (b) They should do the things they had learned, received, heard, and seen in him. (c) faith; longsuffering; love; perseverance

32. (a) the things that promote peace and edification; (b) the unity of the Spirit in the bond of peace

33. give a reason for our faith in Christ

34. He will crush Satan under our feet shortly.

Study 13: The Whole Armor of God, Part 2

35. (a) the shield of faith; (b) to quench all the fiery darts of the wicked one

36. (a) the substance of things hoped for and the evidence of things not seen; (b) by faith, not by sight

37. justification before God (and, therefore, peace with Him) and continual access to His grace

38. by hearing the Word of God

39. (1) by casting down arguments and every "high thing" that exalts itself against the knowledge of God; (2) by bringing every thought into captivity to the obedience of Christ

40. Jesus said that if they had faith like a mustard seed, they could say to a mulberry tree, *"Be pulled up by the roots and be planted in the sea,"* and it would obey them.

41. the helmet of salvation

42. (a) hope; (b) anchor; sure; steadfast

43. by confessing our faith in Jesus Christ and believing that God raised Him from the dead

44. (a) Upon our faith, we need to build virtue, knowledge, self-control, perseverance, godliness, brotherly kindness, and love. (b) shortsighted, even blind, living as if he had not been cleansed from his old sins

45. Jesus is able to save us to the *"uttermost,"* because He continually makes intercession for us before God in heaven.

46. the sword of the Spirit, which is the Word of God

47. (a) sharper than any two-edged sword; (b) It can divide soul* from spirit and also reveal the thoughts and intentions of the heart.

48. The judgments of the Lord* are true and completely righteous; the entirety of God's Word is truth.

49. faith

50. *"in season and out of season"*—in other words, all the time

51. (a) (1) delight in it; (2) continually mediate on it; (b) good and evil; (c) by rightly *"dividing,"* or *"handling,"* His Word of truth

52. (a) the armor of light; (b) the Lord Jesus Christ

53. (a) the light of the world; (b) (1) they do not walk in darkness; (2) they have the light of life

Study 14: Prayer, Fasting, and Praise

1. (a) pray always with all prayer and supplication in the Spirit; (b) being watchful to fulfill this purpose with all perseverance as they prayed for other believers

2. earnestly; vigilant; serious

3. Pray in private, rather than to be seen by others, and avoid meaningless repetition of words.

4. (a) with the belief that we will receive what we pray for; (b) thanksgiving

5. forgiving those who have wronged us

6. (a) (1) Your kingdom come. (2) Your will be done on earth as it is in heaven. (3) Give us day by day our daily bread. (4) Forgive us our sins, for we also forgive everyone who

is indebted to us. (5) Do not lead us into temptation. (6) Deliver us from the evil one. (b) He told them to pray that they would not enter into temptation.

7. (a) to enable us to lead quiet and peaceable lives in all godliness and reverence; (b) all people being saved and coming to the knowledge of the truth

8. someone who would make a "wall" and stand in the gap before Him on behalf of the land, so that He wouldn't have to destroy it

9. (a) those that correspond with His will; (b) that we have whatever we asked Him for

10. the "prince of the kingdom of Persia" had fought against the angel and held him up from delivering the message from God that was the answer to Daniel's prayer

11. Luke 18:1b: Always pray and not lose heart.

   Romans 12:12b: Continue steadfastly in prayer.

   2 Thessalonians 5:17: Pray without ceasing.

12. that his prayers and his alms, or gifts to the poor, had risen as a memorial before God

13. Hebrews 7:22, 25: Jesus

   Romans 8:26–27: the Holy Spirit

14. (a) (1) with the spirit; (2) with the understanding; (b) the Holy Spirit

15. fell upon; poured out; came upon

16. the effective, fervent prayer of a righteous person

17. (1) What they ask in prayer will be done for them. (2) Jesus will be in their midst.

18. (a) holy hands; (b) wrath and doubting

19. principalities, powers, the rulers of the darkness of this age, and spiritual hosts of wickedness in the heavenly places

20. that they may stand perfect and complete in all of God's will

21. when; then they will fast

22. (a) They put a painful expression on their faces so that everyone will know they are fasting. (b) Father; secret place; (c) He will reward us openly.

23. He fasted for forty days and nights.

24. *"This kind does not go out except by prayer and fasting."*

25. (a) all the Jews in Shushun, as well as her own maids; (b) By royal decree, the Jews were allowed to defend themselves against their enemies, who previously had been given

royal sanction to kill them and take their property. They destroyed their enemies, and their lives were preserved.

26. (a) He was the king's cupbearer. (b) He fasted and prayed before the God of heaven. (c) (1) great; awesome; (2) sins; You; (3) word; You commanded

27. The king was pleased to send Nehemiah to Judah for a predetermined length of time, and he granted his request for safe passage and supplies.

28. (a) fasting and praying; (b) Cornelius's alms, or gifts to the poor

29. (a) a "fast" in which we deliver the oppressed, feed the hungry, house the homeless, clothe the naked, and take care of our own families; (b) We will have light, healing, righteousness, the presence of God's glory, and answered prayer.

30. (a) praise; (b) He would be saved from his enemies.

31. Many would come to trust in the Lord*.

32. (1) blowing trumpets of rams' horns; (2) shouting

33. (a) to sing to the Lord* and to praise the beauty of His holiness*; (b) *Praise the LORD, for His mercy endures forever.* (c) The Lord* sent ambushes against their enemies, and they were defeated.

34. praying and singing hymns to God

35. the garment of praise

36. the sacrifice of praise

Study 15: The Name of Jesus

1. that He would save His people from their sins

2. Isaiah 9:6b: Wonderful, Counselor, Mighty God, Everlasting Father, Prince of Peace
   Malachi 4:2a: the Sun of Righteousness

   John 1:29b: the Lamb of God

   John 6:35a: the bread of life

   John 10:11: the good shepherd

   John 14:6a: the way, the truth, and the life

   Revelation 22:13, 16b: the Alpha and the Omega, the Beginning and the End, the First and the Last; the Root and the Offspring of David; the Bright and Morning Star

3. God the Father

4. all authority in heaven and on earth, and the name that is above every name

5. (a) salvation; (b) (1) the Holy Spirit (Helper); (2) life

6. Luke 9:1 demons and diseases; Luke 10:19: serpents, scorpions, and all the power of the enemy

7. Whatever we bind on earth will be bound in heaven, and whatever we loose on earth will be loosed in heaven.

8. (a) that I will do; I will do it; (b) that the Father may be glorified in the Son*

9. bearing spiritual fruit and maintaining that fruit

10. they will cast out demons, speak with new tongues, take up serpents, be unaffected by any deadly substance they might drink, and heal the sick through the laying on of hands

11. Acts 16:16–18; 19:11–12: Paul cast a demon out of a slave girl; evil spirits came out of people who had contact with handkerchiefs and aprons that Paul had touched.

    Acts 2:1–4; 10:44–46a: On the day of Pentecost, Jesus' followers were filled with the Spirit and spoke in tongues; new believers spoke in tongues after the Holy Spirit "fell upon" them.

    Acts 28:3–6: Paul was bitten by a poisonous viper and had no ill effects.

    Acts 3:1–8; Acts 28:8: Peter and John healed a lame man; Paul laid hands on the father of Publius, who was sick with a fever and dysentery, and he was healed.

12. faith in Jesus' name

13. (a) uneducated; untrained; (b) they had been with Jesus

14. Jesus told John not to forbid the man to cast out demons, because he was not against them but was "on their side."

15. (a) *Jesus I know, and Paul I know; but who are you?* (b) Fear fell on all of them, and they magnified the name of Jesus.

16. (a) They were commanded not to speak or teach in the name of Jesus; they were threatened; they were beaten; they were imprisoned; they were put to death. (b) (1) They said they couldn't help speaking the things that they had seen and heard. (2) They prayed that God would give them boldness to continue to speak His Word and to do healings, signs, and wonders in the name of Jesus. (c) *We ought to obey God rather than men.*

17. Everyone who loses houses or family members or lands for His name's sake will receive back a hundredfold, as well as inherit eternal life.

18. the name of the Lord our God

19. (a) as a strong tower; (b) they are safe

20. hold fast to My name; did not deny My faith

21. *"And whatever you do in word or deed, do all in the name of the Lord Jesus."*

Study 16: The Blood of the Lamb

1. new covenant

2. not well; they did not keep God's covenant and refused to walk in His law; their hearts were not steadfast with God

3. to cleanse the people from their sins

4. (a) did not continue in; (b) not possible; take away sins; (c) never; make; perfect

5. (a) once for all; (b) one sacrifice; perfected forever

6. God said He would put His laws into our hearts and write them in our minds. He also would not remember our sins and lawless deeds.

7. a one-year-old male lamb (a sheep or a goat) without blemish

8. The blood would be a sign, protecting the Israelites from God's judgment in the plague that would destroy all the firstborn of Egypt; He would "pass over" those who had applied the blood.

9. *"Christ, our Passover, was sacrificed for us."*

10. without blemish

11. He described Jesus as a lamb without blemish or spot.

12. Although Jesus was tempted in all ways, He never sinned.

13. (a) life; in the blood; (b) makes atonement; (c) no remission

14. Jesus' blood justifies us, so that we are saved from wrath

15. through faith

16. an everlasting covenant

17. Colossians 1:19–20: He has reconciled all things to God.

    Revelation 5:9b: He has redeemed human beings to God out of every tribe, tongue, people, and nation on earth.

18. enter the "Holiest"

19. (a) dead works; (b) serve the living God

20. salvation; strength; the kingdom of our God; the power of Christ

21. It cleanses us from all sin.

22. There is no condemnation to those who are in Christ Jesus, who walk according to the Spirit. We have been freed from the law of sin and death.

23. (a) the image of prisoners being set free from a waterless pit; (b) *"Return to the stronghold ["your fortress" NIV]"*; (c) that He would restore double to them

24. power, riches, wisdom, strength, honor, glory, and blessing

Study 17: The Word of Our Testimony

1. faithful and true

2. what He has seen and heard

3. the truth

4. everyone who is of the truth

5. They bore witness of Him, that God the Father had sent Him.

6. (a) the commandments of God; (b) the testimony of Jesus Christ

7. God has given us eternal life, and this life is in His Son.

8. Those who had heard Him (Jesus) confirmed His words.

9. heard; seen; looked upon; handled

10. the Helper, the Spirit of truth (the Holy Spirit)

11. that we are children of God

12. (a) as servants of Christ and stewards of the mysteries of God; (b) that they be found faithful/faithfulness

13. through signs and wonders, various miracles, and gifts of the Holy Spirit

14. (a) their faith; (b) his faith, through which he offered God a more excellent sacrifice than Cain; (c) his faith

15. (a) faith; (b) word of the Lord*; faith

16. (a) God's righteousness and God's lovingkindness and truth; (b) God's faithfulness and salvation

17. (a) a defense to everyone who asks us a reason for the hope that is in us; (b) with meekness/gentleness, fear/respect, and a good conscience

18. (a) what they should say to these leaders and how they should say it; (b) speak whatever the Holy Spirit and Jesus give them to say at that time

19. because it is the power of God to salvation for everyone who believes—both Jews and Greeks

20. with grace, seasoned with salt

21. bishops/overseers and deacons

22. (a) We should gently, patiently, and humbly correct those who are in opposition, in hopes that God will grant them repentance, so that they may know the truth, come to their senses, and escape the snare of the devil. (b) his will; (c) reject him; He is warped and in sin and thereby has condemned himself

23. (a) having a form of godliness but denying its power; (b) the truth; (c) corrupt

24. outcome; conduct

25. (a) good works; (b) dead

26. feeding the hungry and refreshing the thirsty; showing hospitality/giving shelter to strangers; clothing the naked; visiting the sick and imprisoned; helping orphans and widows

27. Whoever confesses Him before men will be confessed by Him before His Father in heaven. Whoever denies Him before men will be denied by Him before His Father in heaven.

28. (a) They have been slain for the Word of God and for the testimony they held. (b) They did not love their lives to the death.

29. (a) (1) those who kill the body but cannot kill the soul*; (2) Him who is able to destroy both soul* and body in hell; (b) He said that our heavenly Father knows when even a sparrow falls to the ground, and that we are much more valuable to Him than sparrows. The very hairs on our heads are numbered by Him.

30. the spirit of power, love, and a sound mind

31. He remains faithful because He cannot deny Himself.

32. by walking in the light of Jesus; by confessing our sins, receiving God's forgiveness, and being cleansed from all unrighteousness

33. (a) the testimony of Christ; (b) Jesus Christ

34. by living without complaining and disputing, so that we may become blameless and harmless, children of God without fault, standing out in the midst of a generation characterized by crookedness and perverseness

Part V: Final Victory

Study 18: A Good Soldier of Jesus Christ

1. brother; worker; soldier

2. (a) fight the good fight of faith; (b) eternal life

3. by not becoming entangled with the affairs of this life, or civilian affairs

4. no reputation; bondservant; humbled Himself; became obedient

5. They choke the Word of God in a person's life and cause him to be unfruitful.

6. They will give heed to deceiving spirits and doctrines of demons.

7. (1) Seek first the kingdom of God and His righteousness. (2) Love the Lord* with all your heart, soul*, mind, and strength. (3) Love your neighbor as yourself.

8. (a) by "abiding" in Jesus; (b) nothing; (c) a withered branch that is thrown into a fire for burning

9. (a) (1) take heed; (2) watch; (3) pray; (b) (1) soberly/self-controlled; (2) righteously/upright; (3) godly

10. (a) circumspectly; redeeming the time; (b) by understanding what the will of the Lord* is

11. endure hardship

12. count the cost

13. suffering persecution

14. (a) to work out their own salvation with fear and trembling; (b) obeyed; (c) that God is working in us both to will and to do for His good pleasure

15. (a) a far more exceeding and eternal weight of glory; (b) the things that are seen, because they are temporary; (c) the things that are not seen, because they are eternal

16. (a) have received; so walk in Him; (b) built up; established; thanksgiving

17. (a) He told Paul that His grace was sufficient for him, because His strength is made perfect in weakness. (b) so that the power of Christ might rest on Him; (c) *"For when I am weak, then I am strong."*

18. (a) restore him in a spirit of gentleness, considering ourselves, so that we won't be tempted; (b) by bearing one another's burdens

19. He should bear with the other person's *"scruples,"* or *"failings"*; he should not please himself but rather the other person, for the person's good, which will lead to his edification.

20. a soul* is saved from death, and a multitude of sins are covered

21. that all things will work together for good to them

22. (a) He will never leave or forsake us. (b) *"The LORD is my helper; I will not fear. What can man do to me?"*

23. (a) the world; (b) our faith

24. to be steadfast, immovable, always abounding in the work of the Lord*, knowing that our labor in Him is not in vain

25. deliver us

26. to count us worthy of our calling and to fulfill all the good pleasure of His goodness and the work of faith with power; (b) The name of the Lord Jesus Christ will be glorified in us, and we will be glorified in Him, according to the grace of God and the Lord Jesus Christ.

Study 19: The End of the Age and the Last Battle

1. They will say something like, "I thought He promised to return. So, where is He?"

2. one day; thousand years

3. God is longsuffering, or patient, toward people. He is not willing that anyone should perish but that all should come to repentance and salvation.

4. *"Fear God and give glory to Him, for the hour of His judgment has come; and worship Him who made heaven and earth, the sea and springs of water."*

5. (a) No. (Only God the Father knows.) (b) We should not believe it or go out to look. (c) Matthew 24:27: lightning flashing from the east to the west; 2 Peter 3:10a: a thief in the night

6. power; great glory

7. (a) with a shout, with the voice of an archangel, and with the trumpet of God. (b) the dead in Christ; (c) They will be caught up together in the clouds with the dead who have been raised, to meet the Lord* in the air.

8. (a) Verses 6–7: wars and rumors of wars; nations rising up against nation and kingdom against kingdom; famines, pestilences, earthquakes

   Verse 9: believers undergoing tribulation and death, being hated by all nations for the sake of the name of Christ

   Verse 10: people being offended and betraying and hating one another

   Verse 11: many false prophets rising up to deceive many

   Verse 12: the love of many growing cold because of lawlessness

(b) he who endures to the end; (c) The gospel of the kingdom will be preached in the whole world as a witness to the nations.

9. False christs and false prophets will rise up and show great signs and wonders, to the extent that even the elect could be deceived, if that were possible

10. watch and be diligent to be found by Christ "in peace," without spot and blameless

11. (1) the falling away; (2) the revealing of the *"man of sin,"* the *"son of perdition"*

12. He will oppose all that is called God or that is worshipped. He will exalt himself, sitting as God in God's temple and thereby claiming to be God.

13. John said that if these antichrists had been a part of them, they would have continued with them. Since they "went out," or left, they manifested the fact that they were not a part of them.

14. 1 John 2:22: that Jesus is the Christ; the Father and the Son*

    1 John 4:2–3: that Jesus Christ has come in the flesh*

15. (a) his power, his throne, and great authority; (b) the dragon (Satan) and the beast; (c) *"Who is like the beast? Who is able to make war with him?"*; (d) those whose names are written in Book of Life of the Lamb slain from the foundation of the world

16. (a) blasphemy against God, His name, His tabernacle, and those who dwell in heaven; (b) to make war with the saints and to overcome them; (c) every tribe, tongue, and nation

17. Verse 13: perform great signs, such as making fire come down to the earth from heaven

    Verse 14: deceive people by these signs and tell people on earth to make an image to the (first) beast

    Verse 15: give breath to the image of the beast, so that the image itself speaks, and cause those who will not worship the image of the beast to be killed

    Verses 16–17: cause all the people on earth to receive a mark on their right hands or on their foreheads, so that no one can buy or sell unless they have the mark of the beast, the name of the beast, or the number of his name

18. (a) to gather them to battle against God Almighty; (b) Armageddon

19. overcome them

20. (1) called; (2) chosen; (3) faithful

21. (a) with eyes like a flame of fire, with many crowns on His head, wearing a robe dipped in blood, having the name "The Word of God," and having a name that He alone knows

22. (a) righteousness; (b) a sharp sword (coming out of His mouth); (c) KING OF KINGS AND LORD OF LORDS; (d) the armies of heaven, clothed in fine linen, white and clean

23. (a) captured and cast alive into the lake of fire; (b) killed with the sword of Christ, and their flesh* consumed by birds

24. a thousand years

25. those who were beheaded for their witness to Jesus and for the word of God, who had not worshipped the beast or his image and had not received his mark on their foreheads or hands

26. (a) Fire will come down from God out of heaven and devour them. (b) Satan will be cast into the lake of fire and brimstone, where the beast and false prophet are, to be tormented forever.

27. (a) the Lord Jesus Christ; (b) according to what we did while we were on earth—our works, whether good or bad

28. the word that Jesus spoke

29. the secrets of men; the hidden things of darkness and the counsels of people's hearts

30. (1) the world; (2) angels

31. the keys of Hades (hell) and death

32. Verse 14: Death and Hades

    Verse 15: anyone not found written in the Book of Life

33. (a) enemies under His feet; (b) the kingdom

Study 20: When the War Is Over

1. The dead will be raised incorruptible. Those who are still alive will be changed and will "put on" immortality.

2. (a) pass away; melt; burned up; (b) new heavens and a new earth in which righteousness dwells; (c) with men (mankind)

3. (a) God's face; (b) God's name; (c) He would know just as he also is known.

4. make all things new

5. death, sorrow, crying, and pain

6. (a) as the holy city of Jerusalem, descending out of heaven from God and having His glory; (b) as a precious stone, like a jasper stone, clear as crystal

7. (a) twelve fruits; (b) the healing of the nations

8. Revelation 21:23: because the glory of God will illuminate the city, and the Lamb will be its light

   Revelation 22:5: because the Lord God will give the people light, and there will be no night there

9. *"Then the righteous will shine forth as the sun in the kingdom of their Father."*

10. (1) jasper; (2) pure gold, like clear glass; (3) all kinds of precious stones; (4) twelve pearls: each individual gate was of one pearl; (5) pure gold, like transparent glass

11. the reward of the inheritance

12. (a) blessed; inherit; kingdom; foundation; (b) Whatever they did for one of the least of His brethren, they did to Him.

13. *"Well done, good and faithful servant; you were faithful over a few things, I will make you ruler over many things. Enter into the joy of your lord."*

14. kings and priests

15. (a) on the earth; (b) forever and ever

16. without fear, in holiness* and righteousness before Him all the days of our lives

17. all things

18. *"I will be his God and he shall be My son."*

19. (a) those who do (obey) Jesus' commandments; (b) the tree of life; (c) through the gates and into the city (New Jerusalem)

20. "Come!"

21. whoever is thirsty and desires it

22. Jesus

23. (a) They shall never perish, and no one will snatch them out of His hand. (b) those who believe in Jesus and who by patient continuance in doing good seek glory, honor, and immortality

24. to know the only true God and Jesus Christ, whom He has sent

25. quickly

26. keep ourselves in the love of God, looking for the mercy of our Lord Jesus Christ

Glossary

(Note: Throughout this course, references to "God" that have no further designation refer specifically to God the Father, the first person of the Trinity of Father, Son, and Holy Spirit.)

Creator:	God the Father; also, Jesus as the Word through whom all things were created (see John 1:1–3)
flesh:	Sometimes refers to the physical human body but usually to the fallen, sinful nature
Godhead (in the sense of Romans 1:20):	divine nature, deity
holiness:	awesomeness; purity
holy:	awesome; pure
Lord:	In the Old Testament, this term usually refers to God the Father; in the New Testament, the term sometimes refers to Jesus
sanctify:	to make pure, holy*
sanctification:	the process by which the Holy Spirit purifies our minds and hearts and makes us holy*, in the likeness of Jesus
soul:	generally, the mind, will, and emotions; sometimes used as a synonym for the human spirit
spirit (lowercased):	the essential nature of human beings, made in God's image
Spirit of God:	Holy Spirit
Son, the:	Jesus
triune:	three in one

About the Author

Dr. Mary K. Baxter was in full-time ministry for over thirty years, ever since she was taken by God into the dimensions and torments of hell, as well as the streets of heaven, for over forty nights in 1976. God commissioned Mary to record her experiences and tell others of the horrific depths, degrees, and torments of hell, as well as the wonderful destiny of heaven for the redeemed of Jesus Christ. There truly is a hell to shun and a heaven to gain!

Throughout her life, Mary experienced many visions, dreams, and revelations of heaven, hell, and the spirit realm. She was sent by God to minister in over 120 nations, and her books were translated into more than twenty languages. Salvation sprang forth as she walked in the miraculous power of God on her life. Signs and wonders followed her, and testimonies of God's saving grace abounded in her ministry. She had a mother's heart to see all people come into the kingdom of God and become all that God has created them to be. She birthed numerous other ministries and poured into the lives of others to see the kingdom of God expand into the emerging generations of the earth.

Mary was ordained as a minister in 1983 and received a Doctor of Ministry degree from Faith Bible College, an affiliate of Oral Roberts University. She traveled the world and ministered in power. Mary was a best-selling author, and her previous books with Whitaker House include *A Divine Revelation of Hell, A Divine Revelation of Heaven, A Divine Revelation of the Spirit Realm, A Divine Revelation of Angels, A Divine Revelation of Spiritual Warfare, A Divine Revelation of Deliverance, A Divine Revelation of Healing, A Divine Revelation of Prayer,* and *The Power of the Blood.* Mary passed away in 2021.